# I Had the Right to Remain Silent . . .

## But I Didn't Have the Ability

# I Had the Right to Remain Silent . . .
## But I Didn't Have the Ability

Ron White

Illustrations by Matthew Shultz

DUTTON

DUTTON
Published by Penguin Group (USA) Inc.
375 Hudson Street, New York, New York 10014, U.S.A.
Penguin Group (Canada), 90 Eglinton Avenue East, Suite 700, Toronto, Ontario
M4P 2Y3, Canada (a division of Pearson Penguin Canada Inc.); Penguin Books Ltd,
80 Strand, London WC2R 0RL, England; Penguin Ireland, 25 St Stephen's Green,
Dublin 2, Ireland (a division of Penguin Books Ltd); Penguin Group (Australia),
250 Camberwell Road, Camberwell, Victoria 3124, Australia (a division of Pear-
son Australia Group Pty Ltd); Penguin Books India Pvt Ltd, 11 Community Centre,
Panchsheel Park, New Delhi–110 017, India; Penguin Group (NZ), cnr Airborne
and Rosedale Roads, Albany, Auckland 1310, New Zealand (a division of Pearson
New Zealand Ltd); Penguin Books (South Africa) (Pty) Ltd, 24 Sturdee Avenue,
Rosebank, Johannesburg 2196, South Africa

Penguin Books Ltd, Registered Offices: 80 Strand, London WC2R 0RL, England

Published by Dutton, a member of Penguin Group (USA) Inc.

First printing, June 2006
10 9 8 7 6 5 4 3 2

REGISTERED TRADEMARK—MARCA REGISTRADA

LIBRARY OF CONGRESS CATALOGING-IN-PUBLICATION DATA
White Ron, 1956–
    I had the right to remain silent . . . but I didn't have the ability / by Ron White.
        p. cm.
    ISBN 0-525-94961-5 (hardcover)
    1. White, Ron, 1956– 2. Comedians—United States—Biography. I. Title.
PN2287.W45823A3 2006
792.702'8092—dc22                                        2006009056

Printed in the United States of America
Set in Oranda
Designed by Jaime Putorti

While the author has made every effort to provide accurate telephone numbers
and Internet addresses at the time of publication, neither the publisher nor the
author assumes any responsibility for errors, or for changes that occur after publication. Further, the publisher does not have any control over and does not assume any responsibility for author or third-party Web sites or their content.

To my wife, Barbara,
and my son, Marshall

# CONTENTS

# I Had the Right to Remain Silent . . .

## But I Didn't Have the Ability

# 1

# INTRODUCTION

I've put out a CD, *Drunk in Public*; a DVD, *They Call Me "Tater Salad"*; and most recently a CD and DVD, *You Can't Fix Stupid*. But people have also been asking me to do a book. So here it is. Along with comedy I do on-stage, it features some stories of my life as a comedian on, and off, the road.

If you want to give me some feedback on the book, you can e-mail me through my Web site, www.tater salad.com. I'd love to hear from you.

Thanks for reading. I hope you enjoy it.

# 2

# ONSTAGE:
## SET 1

I'm going to start off by asking a question, 'cause I don't know the answer. I lost my sunglasses, and I went to the Sunglass Hut. Here's the question: Why does a pair of sunglasses cost more than a 25-inch color television set? Anybody know?

I go to the Sunglass Hut. I see a pair of glasses I like. I don't love 'em. I like 'em. 309 bucks. And I asked the guy very politely, "How do you sleep at night, you fuckin' prick?"

And I told him, and this is true, that two weeks ago I bought a 25-inch color television set from Wal-Mart for 218 bucks.

And he goes, "Well apparently, sir, you don't get it."

"I'm listening."

He goes, "These glasses eliminate one hundred percent of all UV rays."

I'm like, "No, apparently *you* don't get it. This thing decodes a digital satellite signal it picks up from outer fucking space."

And then it turned out the glasses got basic cable, and I felt like a dickhead.

You ever take a crap so big, your pants fit better? I'm hoping that happens to me soon. I'm hoping I'm one big turd away from backing into an old wardrobe.

7

One day I was sitting in a beanbag chair naked, eating Cheetos, and I was flipping through the television, and I saw Robert Tilton, he's a televangelist from Dallas. And he was staring at me.

And he said this. He said, "Are you lonely?"

*Yeah.*

He said, "Have you wasted half your life in bars, pursuing sins of the flesh?"

*This guy's good.*

He said, "Are you sitting in a beanbag chair naked, eating Cheetos?"

*Yes, sir.*

He said, "Do you feel the urge to get up and send me a thousand dollars?"

*Close.*

I thought he was talking about me there for a second. Apparently I ain't the only cat on the block who digs Cheetos.

I was performing at the State Theatre in Kalamazoo, Michigan, and these guys took me to a blues festival they have near there. And I love the blues, but they need to figure out some problems with the festival. I don't like to party anywhere where you can't just give somebody money and they give you back a beer, you know what I mean?

I stood in line for an hour. My mouth is dry. I want a beer. I love beer. I know they're selling beer. People are walking away from the front of the line, and they've got beer. That's how I figured the whole thing out. I get up there. I give the guy my money.

He goes, "We don't take money here."

"What do you take?"

"Coupins."

"What?"

"Coupins."

"Where do I get a coupin?"

"See that line over there?"

It takes forever. I stood in that line for an hour. I gotta show them my driver's license, birth certificate, fill out a form. They mail that away. Send me back some coupins.

"What are you doing, Ron?"

"I'm waiting on UPS. There's a good chance I'll have a beer by Thursday. I'm partying like a Kennedy right now."

I was game, too. I had 100 bucks cash on me, I bought 100 bucks worth of coupins.

And then some of the guys that took me there asked me if I wanted to go to a topless club. And I didn't, really, want to go . . .

I just ended up going, 'cause—you guys back me up on this—you've seen one woman naked . . . you want to see the rest of them naked. It can be an old biker chick you know they're going to hang down to here.

"You want to see my titties?"

"Yeah, I do . . . All right, that's enough. Roll them back up, sweetheart."

And then closing time came around and the tabs came out, and I found out the titty bar don't accept them coupins.

The guy at Taco Bell told me to kiss his ass.

"I'll give you forty dollars' worth of coupins for a burrito with cheese. It's all I've got. It's a coupin."

I saw something that comes close to truth in advertising. The De Beers people are almost saying what they really mean. Because the old De Beers slogan was, "Diamonds are forever." Then they changed it to, "This year, take her breath away." The new slogan is, "Diamonds, render her speechless."

Why don't they just go ahead and say it? "Diamonds: That'll shut her up. For a minute."

I did a show one night in Cincinnati, and I came off-stage and I was looking for something to eat. And across the street from the club is a place called Skyline Chili. Next door to that's a place called Gold Star Chili, across from that is Liberty Chili, Ray's Chili, Joe's Chili, Bob's Chili, chili everywhere.

Now, I wasn't trying to start any shit with the little chili boy. I was making late-night conversation, and I said to this guy, "You know, it seems like there's a whole lot of chili places here. You wouldn't think there would be, would you?"

And he goes, "I'll have you know the Cincinnati area is the chili capital of the *woild*."

Oh, excuse me for thinking it might be Mexico City or Guadala Goddamn Jara. I don't even think you all told the Mexican boys you were having a contest.

That's right. 'Cause a Mexican boy'd come up here with a goat and an onion and kick your ass. He wouldn't even need a car; he could ride the goat up there.

Of course, he'd need a lift home. Can't ride home on a bowl 'a goat. I've always said that.

I was in Miami when Hurricane Georges hit the Keys a couple years ago. I just thought this was funny. They evacuated the Keys and everybody left except for one guy.

I've been through two hurricanes. I was in Hurricane Carla when I was a kid in Houston. And I was real excited during hurricane time, you know, 'cause I'm out there in the Gulf and it's dangerous. And I'm like, "This is cool."

Till shit started hitting our house. And I was like, "Fuck this."

But anyway they evacuate the Keys and everybody leaves except for one guy, who was gonna stay there and tie himself to a tree on the beach to prove a point.

And the point was, he said, that at fifty-three years of age he was in good enough physical condition to withstand the wind and the rain from a force three hurricane.

All right. Let me explain something to you. It isn't *that* the wind is blowing, it's *what* the wind is blowing.

If you get hit with a Volvo, it doesn't really matter how many sit-ups you did that morning. If you have a yield sign in your spleen, joggin' don't come into play.

"I can run twenty-five miles without stopping."

"You're bleedin'."

"Shit."

That same time in Florida, somebody broke into my truck and stole my radio, thank you, whoever you were.

I got to drive back to Texas listening to the sound of wind for forty-nine hours.

I went to the insurance company. I was filling out these forms. And I got to the part on the form where it says what kind of radio it was. And I told the guy I didn't remember.

And he said, "Mr. White, if you can remember what kind of radio it was, we'll know how much money we can give you."

That's some good news right there. I thought of a real expensive-sounding brand, and I wrote it down. And he knew I was lying.

"Mr. White, I don't believe Rolex makes a radio."

"It was a clock radio. Write the check, Premium Boy."

They love it when you call them Premium Boy. Next time you see your insurance agent, call him Premium Boy. You'll get a chuckle.

I almost died last year. Actually I didn't almost die, I didn't even get hurt.

I was in a near-miss plane crash. And I was flying from Flagstaff, Arizona, to Phoenix, Arizona, because my manager doesn't own a globe.

I was on a plane yay big—like a pack of gum with eight people in it—and the engine going *rrrrrr*, like a playing card on a kid's bike.

We took off from the Flagstaff Airport Hair Care and Tire Center there. We're traveling at half the speed of smell. We got passed by a kite. There was a goose behind us, and the pilot was screaming, "Go around!"

We get halfway to Phoenix, we got to go back. It's a nine-minute flight; can't pull it off with this equipment.

We had engine trouble. We lost some oil pressure in one of the engines and they told us about it over the speaker system of the plane, which was stupid. . . . They could have just leaned back and mumbled, "Hey, we lost some oil pressure."

"Heard ya. Sure did."

It was weird. Everybody on the plane was nervous, but I'd been drinking since lunch and I was like, "Take it down, I don't care."

You ever have one of those days? "Hit something hard. I don't want to limp away from this piece of shit."

The guy sitting next to me is losing his mind. Apparently, he had a lot to live for. He goes, "Hey man, huh, huh, hey man, huh, huh, if one of these engines fails, huh, huh, how far will the other one take us?"

"All the way to the scene of the crash, which is pretty handy, 'cause that's where we're headed. I bet we beat the paramedics there by a half hour. We're hauling ass."

As a stand-up comedian, I've got a really good job. I like my job.

It's important to have a good vocabulary in my job. And actually I haven't always had one. When I was younger, if I'd known the difference between *antidote* and *anecdote*, my friend Bob Schneider would still be alive today.

He got bit by a copperhead; I'm reading him humorous stories out of *Reader's Digest*.

His head's starting to swell. I'm like, "It ain't working."

He goes, "Read faster."

I'll tell ya a little bit about myself. I'm from Texas. I'm a cowboy, a real cowboy. I was a bronc rider for six years of my life, and it's affected me.

Now when I have sex, I have to throw out my arm for balance. Seems to be some dispute between the wife and me, whether or not I'm staying on that *full* eight seconds.

So we got the timer and buzzer, and set it up right there in the bedroom. I taught her the meaning of the phrase "most of the time."

Would've been "all the time," but she won't let me tie that rope around her waist anymore. She hates it when I spur her out of the chute.

Hey, you laugh, it's not easy to keep an erection with a clown in a barrel in the corner of the room.

You gotta stay focused.

I'm probably not a typical Texan in that I don't hunt. I fish, but I don't hunt. And not because I think it might somehow be more holy to eat meat that's been bludgeoned to death by somebody else, that's not it. It's really early in the morning, it's really cold outside, and I don't want to fuckin' go.

My cousin Ray on the other hand thinks killing a deer with a deer rifle is magic in the forest. Here's Ray after the big kill:

"Hell, it was four in the morning, twenty-two degrees outside.

" 'Course, you weren't there . . . pussy. I'm in a camouflaged deer blind with greasepaint on my face. I've got deer urine on my boots—I'm not sure why."

I made that last part up.

"I got a thirty-ought-six with a twelve-power scope and a bullet that'll travel twenty-two hundred feet per second. When that deer looked up and licked the salt sucker I'd hung from the danged oak tree, I caught him right above the eye."

Yeah, well I hit one with a van going 55 miles an hour with the headlights on and the horn blowing. Whoo, that's an elusive little creature.

If you ever miss one, it's 'cause the bullet's moving too fast. Slow the bullet down to 55 miles an hour and put some headlights and a little horn on it. The deer will actually jump in front of the bullet.

I got happily married to a rich woman. If you ever have a choice, go ahead.

Actually, that's a lie. She's not rich at all.

Her parents are loaded. And they hate my guts. And I'm waiting for them to die.

And you'll know if they die, too, 'cause you'll never see my fat ass again. I'll be in Palm Beach with my new friends.

"Hand me a beer, Teddy."

My rich in-laws have servants. Is that weird? I thought when I married their daughter, they'd send a servant along with us to help do all the shit they never taught her how to do.

And I was wrong. We're leaning on her domestic skills. Ooh, she's handy.

I came home from doing a show one night, and she goes, "Honey, the dryer's broken."

"Did you check the lint filters, sweetheart? Sit down, honey, I'll check it." I open it up.

"Is there anything in there?"

"There's a *quilt* in there. Look, you made a sofa cushion. You are a handy girlie-whirly."

I hear a lot of, "Ron, you're a pretty good-sized old boy. Well, I guess the little woman's a good cook."

Bullshit. Oh, it got a little better when she figured out that the smoke alarm's not a timer. I had to tell her, "Honey, the food is done before that particular buzzer goes off."

It was real bad when we first got married. The first meal she cooked in our new house, I couldn't eat it. I gave it to my dog, Sluggo. And he started licking his butt.

She comes in the kitchen and goes, "What's he doing?"

"Looks like he's trying to get the taste out of his mouth."

Everything's an emergency to her, because she never had to deal with her own problems. Spoiled, catered to her whole life. There's no cure for that.

I was performing in Atlanta, she called me one night, misses me in the hotel room. They catch me in the lobby and tell me I have an emergency phone call from home.

I knock over ten people in the lobby of a very nice hotel, thinking maybe my in-laws . . .

I call her, she tells me Sluggo just took a dump on the new carpet.

"Shoot him."

She goes, "That's just like you, Ron. I have a genuine problem, and you're being sarcastic."

"All right, honey, I'm sorry. Put the dog on the phone, I'll talk to him."

What do you want me to do? I'm in Georgia. I can't pick up the turd.

"Put a paper towel over it. I'll be home in a week, honey."

I get home, it looks like a little campground in the living room. Somebody's having a Poopapalooza concert.

"Let him outside. He'll shit out there. I've seen him do it."

We have a beautiful son. His name is Marshall. I named him after an amplifier.

I almost named him Peavey. "Come here, Blaupunkt, ya little woofer, get over here."

When my son was five years old, he thought five years old was a very cool age to be. Because that was the coolest age he'd gotten to.

His favorite thing about being five years old was he was old enough to wear a seat belt. That was his biggest physical step toward manhood so far in his eyes, you know. He was strapped in the truck just like his daddy, and he thought that was great.

I thought it was great too, 'cause I drove a four-wheel-drive truck. And I learned this about four-wheel-drive trucks.

It doesn't really matter how big the motor is or how big the tires are, your macho days are over when you strap a baby's car seat in the front of that bad boy. You just can't show it off to your buddies, you know what I mean?

You can't make yourself go, "What's that? That's got the Vortec V8 running two-eighty-five horsepower.

"That? That's a Manitowoc power winch. That'll pull twenty-eight tons right out of the ditch.

"That? That's a Playskool car seat—with the Big Bird steering wheel attachment right there on it. That's Bert on the blinker and Ernie on the windshield wiper. That's Big Bird in the middle, you can honk that fat bastard if you want to. Hell, in two weeks I'll have the Cookie Monster flip mirror, they back-ordered it on me."

I stopped driving the truck to gigs, 'cause I bought this big two-story custom van to tour in. And it was kind of neat. It had the James Bond couch in the back, where you push a button and the couch automatically turns into a bed.

I'm like, "Well, that's cool, I finally got something over those Mercedes-Benz–driving in-laws of mine," you know what I mean? When I first bought the van I was real proud of it, and I took it straight over to my brother-in-law's house to show it off, 'cause he's such a prick.

He takes one look at my new van, and he goes, "I can't believe you didn't buy a Mercedes-Benz."

"They don't make a van."

"Ron, I don't think you fully understand the intricacies of Mercedes-Benz engineering. Why, I've got the three-inch windshield wipers that keep my headlights clean in a rainstorm."

"I got a place to fuck your sister."

I don't know why they didn't like me.

I promised Sears I would tell this story every night on-stage until the lawsuit's settled.

I had the van down in Savannah, Georgia, and I didn't like the way the tires were wearing on it. I took the van to Sears Automotive, "a trusted name in automotive service."

Takes them three and a half hours to change four tires. Apparently they had to whittle one of them out of a piece of wheat.

I pay them $980 of my hard-earned money. I take a right-hand turn out of the mall. The left rear wheel falls off. It falls off! IT FALLS THE FUCK OFF!

Turning my van into a tripod. Spinning me into a dimension of pissed-off I have never been in before in my life!

This guy was a tire guy. That's all he did. He didn't some days work on transmissions. He was a tire guy.

Sears, I found out later, had sent him to tire college for three days. Well apparently, he was sick on LUG NUT DAY! But they still let him work on my van.

So I'm suing 'em, and I hope that next year they have to change the name of Sears Tower in Chicago to Ron White's Big Ole Goddamned Building.

You can all come over and party too. I'm gonna have a lot of room.

"Think we oughta clean up, Ron?"

"Hell no, move to another floor. We'll conga up there. Somebody grab my butt. Bring your coupins."

The thing with Sears wasn't as painful as buying the car in the first place, 'cause I had to talk to a car salesman to get it. Nobody else sells cars.

I believe if somebody asked me, "Uh, Ron, Ron, Ron"—sometimes it's hard to get my attention—"Ron, would you rather spend two hours of your life talking to a car salesman? *Orrrr* would you rather be drug naked over a cactus with your mouth over the tailpipe of a Greyhound bus? *Orrrr* would you rather sandpaper the asshole of an alligator in a phone booth?"

"What was that second one again?"

If you're reading this, and you're a car salesman, I'll show you where you are on the food chain. If the whole universe was a mike stand, about two inches off the ground there would be a flabby hunk of whale shit.

You're below that.

Oh, look right next to you there's a lawyer. Hey, there's my lawyer. There's my first wife. There's her mother.

And there's that asshole that didn't put the lug nuts back on my goddamn van.

Eventually I got happily divorced. I'll tell you what went wrong.

She got convinced in her crazy head that I had sex with this girl in Columbus, Ohio. And I did, and I'll tell ya why.

When you enter into a monogamous relationship with somebody, you usually do it at a point in the relationship when you're having a lot of sex. So you're willing to sign the papers. I'll only have sex with you, ever, ever, ever. Ever.

Well, if that person stops having sex altogether, why, you find yourself in quite a pickle. I'm a pretty good dog, but if you don't pet me every once in a while it's hard to keep me under the porch. I'm not as flexible as a real dog.

I'll tell ya what happened too. I was in Columbus, Ohio, I hadn't been laid in three months. Three months! You can't go three months without having sex with me; I'll go have sex with somebody else. I know, I've seen me do it.

I did a show one night. I came offstage. There was a gorgeous woman, maybe thirty-five, forty years old, long black dress slit up to her waist, *gorgeous*.

She goes, "I thought you were hilarious. I want to buy you a drink."

I'm like, "Aw, I can't do that, I'm married."

She goes, "I didn't ask if you wanted to have sex, big boy, I asked if you wanted to have a drink at my place."

"All right."

Well, you know that little guy that sits on your shoulder that reminds you of your prior commitments and your moral fortitude? I didn't hear a peep out of that guy.

He hadn't been laid in three months either. He was speechless for like twenty minutes, then he was like, "Suck her titty."

I'm like, "I was gonna." I'm having a three-way with my conscience. Soon as the whole thing's over, he's back at his post.

"That was wrong, mister."

"Hey, twenty minutes ago you were beating off on my shoulder, monkey boy."

I hate him. He smokes pot. He burned a hole in my other jacket.

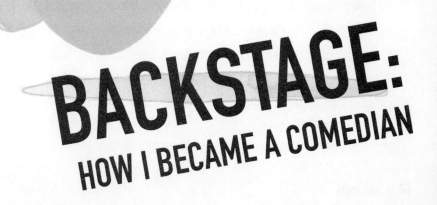

# 3

# BACKSTAGE:
## HOW I BECAME A COMEDIAN

The short answer to how I became a comedian is that nothing else quite worked out. My daddy was a supervisor in a refinery, and a lot of our relatives had jobs in the oil patch. When Dad asked me what I wanted to do when I grew up, I just thought, "Something different."

I was born in a little town called Fritch, Texas, north of Amarillo. But I grew up mostly in and around Houston. So that made a big difference between my father and me, because he was born and raised in a little town, whereas I had all the distractions of a big metropolitan area.

I got into all the usual growing-up behavior and misbehavior—maybe sometimes a little unusual misbehavior, given my problems with impulse control. Like a lot of comedians, I guess I was a bit of an oddball compared to most other kids.

One of my buddies from the time I was about seven years old was the nephew of a professional football player, a linebacker for the Green Bay Packers. I thought it was so cool to know an NFL player in person, and as a result of meeting him, I became a Green Bay Packers fan. Being a Packers fan in Texas during the mid-1960s, when the Dallas Cowboys were having these epic battles with Green Bay, put me in a minority of two with my buddy.

It's really one of the strongest memories of my childhood, realizing how un-OK it was to like the Packers just because you knew one of 'em, if everybody else was against 'em. That started a pattern where on any football game, wherever my family's rooting interest was, I tended to lean the other way.

And I guess I tended to go across the grain in some other ways as well. I never worried what other people were gonna think or what trouble I was gonna wind up in. I just thought, "Oh, hey, that'll be fun." I kind of enjoyed the reactions my behavior—and more than that, my comments—could provoke in people. But I didn't enjoy the trouble I got in with my parents, the neighbors, or my teachers. I was just always looking for something fun to do and not thinking through the implications.

You know that expression "Look before you leap"? I didn't often take a very good look first. And as a result, I wound up leaping into a ton of shit as a boy.

I really had no idea what I was going to do with myself in life. I never thought, "I'm going to be a performer." That wasn't on the list on career day at school.

When I was seventeen I went into the Navy. It was

the very tail end of the Vietnam War, and I was assigned to an ARS—an auxiliary rescue and salvage ship—the USS *Conserver* (ARS-39), commissioned in 1936. It was less than a hundred yards long, and it had a crew of eighty-seven. It was a genuine piece of shit, with eight big old loud Caterpillar engines, slow as it could be. To go from our home port in Pearl Harbor, Hawaii, to Korea it took us thirty-one days. That's with a motor, not a paddle.

We were having a family day picnic on our ship one day in Hawaii, and I didn't have any family coming from Texas for that, so I was on watch. This guy Hoskins was supposed to take the next watch, and I yelled down to him, "Hey, Hoskins, get up here and relieve me before somebody eats all that tater salad."

Hoskins started calling me "Tater Salad," and pretty soon the whole ship was doing it. I kind of thought I was gonna leave that nickname behind in the Navy, but it followed me, as I've talked about onstage.

We also went to the Philippines, Singapore, Hong Kong, and all over the western Pacific. We had great duty in great ports. We went to some neat smaller ports that the big ships couldn't get into. Meanwhile I was seventeen, fat, and stupid, making every mistake I could possibly make.

For a while we were stationed on Grande Island in Subic Bay in the Philippines. That was a big drop-off point for bringing civilian South Vietnamese refugees out of Vietnam. I had a little supply hut where I handed out tampons and toilet paper and toothpaste and so on. I would try to give the tampons to eighty-year-old women, 'cause I didn't know any better, and they would laugh.

My shipmates and I always found ways to amuse ourselves. And I picked up a nasty little drug habit, one I'd put up against anybody's who wasn't a professional musician.

After that I needed a rehab program, and eventually I went into one in Houston. When I completed the program, I went to work for that same program as a counselor, and that led to my becoming one of their primary public speakers. My job was telling my life story onstage in high schools full of kids.

I never saw anybody take to anything as quickly as I took to doing that, three or four times a day. I loved the responses of the kids, and I believe I did 'em some good.

We started getting complaints, though. Some school principals thought my stories shouldn't be so funny. That was the major criticism. I'd say, "Go tell 'em *your* story, and see if they wind up facing in the right direction." But I knew there's no better way to teach somebody something than with a funny story.

That still didn't equate in my mind with making a living doing stand-up. I genuinely didn't get that that was an opportunity for anybody who wanted to try it. After a while I stopped working for the drug treatment program, and I began to do other things, like selling windows.

I was a great point-of-contact salesperson. If you knew you needed windows, and you were sitting there across from me, I could sell you the windows for sure. But you'd usually have to come find me in a titty bar. Figure that in, and I really wasn't all that great at sales. To be a successful salesperson, you've got to have a really strong work ethic.

At that time I was married to Marshall's mother, Terry, although Marshall hadn't been born yet. We were living in Abilene, and I was working for a company that had made big promises, but they had no money. They had no money at all. Instead they had a trade system going with these things called barter units, so we could only eat at two restaurants that would take this not real money. And we were completely broke.

The company kept saying they were gonna get us a check and gonna get us a check. And we owed everybody money. So when they finally did get us a check, we were really excited, we paid all our bills. Then that check bounced, and every check that we wrote bounced, and then we had exactly no money.

So we had to go drive this little Mustang of Terry's to Amarillo to borrow money from my father. And we were so broke that if we got to a downhill we turned off the engine and coasted as long as we could, and then we jump-started the engine again at the bottom of the hill. We borrowed enough money from Dad to rent a truck and pay off most of our bills, but we had to leave our apartment in the middle of the night. This apartment was so tiny that we used to crawl out a window and sit on the roof of the unit next to it at night, 'cause it had no air conditioning.

As we were leaving in the middle of the night— and I know nobody else has ever done this—the two of us couldn't get the couch out the door. We couldn't remember how we got it in, but it was in, so we must have done it. But it was getting light outside, and we actually left our couch hanging in the doorway. We're like, "Let's just go."

We drove this big U-Haul truck full of our stuff to Dallas. And when we got to Dallas, we had no job, we had no place to stay. All our stuff's on a truck that's fifty bucks a day, and we don't have the fifty bucks a day. And we go over to a friend of my wife's who lived in Arlington, and she isn't home.

It's a hundred degrees outside, and we're filthy dirty and sweating from moving and just need a shower and clean clothes. And her house is locked. So we decide we'll go stand in the backyard in the shade. We go in the backyard, and her dog—this big Doberman pinscher—is back there. We know the dog, and as soon as we walk into the backyard, he comes over to me and lifts a leg and just pees all down my leg.

So now we're broke, we're hungry, we're thirsty and filthy, and I'm peed on. We're looking for a place to stay. And we didn't qualify to stay anywhere. Any apartment, even the lowest one, you couldn't say, "Well, I don't have any money, and I don't have a job. And I don't have a prospect of a job. But I'm sure I'll get a job."

We found this little duplex house in Arlington. Two fences down on the back side of the house there was an ax murderer who killed a gas station attendant with a hatchet. It was a really nice area.

Our friends Danny and Sherry Davidson and their dogs lived on one side. And then Terry and I and Sluggo lived on the other side. It was quite comfortable, and we liked living there. And we couldn't afford the place, to tell you the truth. We had to con the land-lord into letting us move in, 'cause we didn't have enough money to float it off 'em week to week.

I started selling storm windows with a fellow named Sam Bartholomew. Sammy and I made our sales calls in his Datsun B210. He weighed 305 pounds, I weighed 270, and this thing would barely get moving. It ran on three cylinders. It wasn't all the same color. It had a fender that was basically just primer and rust. And since Sammy weighed nearly forty pounds more than me, it always leaned a little bit in Sammy's direction.

And we would trudge off down the road—with no money. Sammy was as broke as me. He was comin' out of bankruptcy with a grocery store and he had tax debts.

We were quite a pair. We were just trying to find a way to build a life.

We would go to the highest end part of Dallas, called Highland Park, in the Datsun B210, and try to sell these expensive windows to builders. And at lunch every day we would sit on the hood of his Datsun B210 in front of a 7-Eleven in Highland Park, and eat one 7-Eleven hot dog each.

You know how 7-Eleven stores have a chili dispenser

and a cheese dispenser, and then an onion and relish and mustard thing? And I guess they assume that you're going to use a reasonable amount of these products.

Not if you only have 75 cents for lunch.

We would buy our hot dogs and they would give 'em to us in these paper box containers that they use. And we would take our boxes to the condiments counter, and open them up, and just fill the whole thing up with chili and cheese and onion and relish. You can put three or four pounds of stuff in there if you really want to.

Then we'd walk out trying not to let them see what we'd done. We'd sit on the hood of the Datsun B210 and eat our one hot dog apiece with fixings. And then we'd drink out of a hose at the side of the 7-Eleven.

In 1986 the Funny Bone chain of comedy clubs opened up a club in Arlington, Texas, between where I lived and where I worked. Sammy went to an open-mic night and he came back and said, "Ron, you're funnier than these guys. You need to go over there on open-mic night."

So I scribbled down five minutes of rip-snorting comedy, auditioned for the club manager, and got rejected. But I'm a persistent dog, and I went back on the next open-mic night.

That's when I met Jeff Foxworthy, one of the luckiest things ever to happen to me. Jeff was headlining at the Funny Bone, and he was gracious enough to be there on open-mic night and listen to everybody and then close the night with some stuff of his own.

I did my five minutes, and milked a few laughs out of the audience. My material wasn't really all that good, but I had the basics a comedian needs, a sense of timing, and so on.

When I came offstage the first person I saw was Jeff, and he comes up to me and he says, "Man, you're really funny. But you need to put the punch line at the end of the joke."

I was like, "What?"

He goes, "You need to put the punch line at the end of the joke."

And Jeff sat down with me, a first-time-ever comedian, and he was so generous. He said, "Let's start with your first joke." He wrote it out on a piece of paper, and he said, "You're saying the funny thing here in the middle, and then you still have something else to say. So people are laughing, but you keep talking, and then you have that awkward moment at the end. If you switch things around, you can say the punch line at the end, and then just look at 'em and watch 'em laugh."

I'm like, "No shit."

Today, that's second nature to me. But it's a learned skill. Every comedian has to learn about structuring a joke and a series of jokes and a whole set. As natural as Foxworthy was at that relatively early point in his career—he hadn't been doing stand-up for very long and he was already a headliner—he still had to learn it from other good comedians.

The next day Jeff and I played golf, and we were involved in a vehicular incident. And we really bonded as friends from that point on.

That open-mic experience, with Jeff Foxworthy's feedback to validate me, was the beginning of my life as a journeyman comedian. I traveled all over the South and up through the Midwest in my pickup truck, doing little clubs.

I did that for about three years, working my way up to being the opening act at good clubs like the Improv in Dallas. And I was the opening act there when Sam Kinison came to town to do a sold-out concert for two thousand people at the Dallas Convention Theater. To that point I'd never appeared before more than 350 people.

For some reason, Sam's usual opening act couldn't make it. The promoter called the Improv the day of the show, and asked if they had anybody there who could step in that night. And the people at the Improv asked me if I wanted to take a shot at it.

I was hyperventilating, "Ah, ah, ah, ah—OK."

Sam Kinison's brother was his manager, and he told me, "If it doesn't go well, don't be afraid. A lot of times the audience treats Sam's opening act like a sacrificial lamb. They'll just start screamin' and hollerin' and goin' crazy. If that happens, don't worry about it."

In one way that's kind of encouraging, because nobody's expecting that much from me, and in another way it's not. I didn't know if I was sunk before I went out onstage or what.

I went out there, I did the first joke, and it got a laugh. I did the next joke, and it got a laugh. I'm beginning to enjoy myself.

Now, as an opening-act comedian, I had about twenty minutes of material. I was supposed to do ten minutes before Sam Kinison came out. But I did ten minutes, and he hadn't arrived yet. So I started doing the rest of my stuff as slowly as possible, and I managed to make my act last thirty minutes.

When I came offstage, Sam's bodyguard came up to me and said that Sam wanted to meet me before he went on. Now at the time, in 1989, Sam Kinison was as big a headliner as there was in comedy, and I was a huge fan of his myself. So I was really in awe of him.

They took me to meet him backstage, and he says, "I heard you killed 'em, Cowboy."

I go, "It's a fun crowd."

He says, "Let me show you how to do it." And he went out there and just murdered the audience. He had them screaming with laughter.

After Sam's performance, a lot of people came backstage, including some top people from the Funny Bone chain, the Last Laugh chain, and the Punchline chain of comedy clubs. And one of the guys who owned the Funny Bone said, "Ron, let's go to dinner and talk about your career," which represents a giant break for me.

That's what I'm hearing in one ear. In the other ear, I'm hearing Sam Kinison saying, "C'mon, Cowboy, let's go out in the limo and party."

True to form, I went out in the limo to party with Sam. Luckily for me, the next day the people from the comedy clubs still wanted to talk to me. Almost immediately I was booked for fifty weeks a year as a featured performer in all these chains of comedy clubs at $550 a week. That sounded like retirement money to me then.

So that moved me up another level. But mostly I was still playing in the same comedy clubs all through the Midwest and the South. I had a lot of fun doing that. And my idea anyway was to stay in the Midwest and the South and get as good as I could before I tried to crack the Northeast and the West Coast. Because I knew the headline comedians in Los Angeles and New York were really good, and I didn't want to go in anywhere with half a plate of material.

4

ONSTAGE:
SET 2

I'm a dog lover. Actually, I love *my* dog, I don't give a shit about *your* dog. I don't know your dog. Your dog could be an asshole, I don't know.

My dog, Sluggo, is an English bulldog. Sluggo's like, "Don't jack with me."

You know what I do to him when he's asleep? I lift up those big ole huge bulldog jowls, and I hide M&M's and shit in there. He wakes up in the morning, he's like, *"Slurp-slop-slurp!* It's going to be a good day, Tater." He calls me Tater.

He's a great dog. He's sick right now, which is a pain in the butt, because if he gets sick, you can't just feed him medicine, he'll spit it out. You got to hide it in a piece of cheese.

I stud him out last year for pick of the litter. And I put him with the female dog for a couple of weeks, and then to make sure it took, I took him down to the veterinarian's office and had artificial insemination done twice.

Now for those of you that don't know, that's where they obtain the semen from Sluggo manually, by hand, and put it in the female dog. And now it don't take shit to get old Sluggo to go to the vet. He loves the place.

I went down there. The veterinarian had the audacity to say to me, "Mr. White, if you'll just come on back here, we'll show you how to do this. Next time you don't have to bring in the dog, you can just bring in the semen."

I went, "That's OK. You go ahead and jack off the dog. He follows me around too much as it is."

Like I'm going to spend the rest of my life with this bulldog.

"Don't jack with me, Tater. Jack me off!"

"Get out of here. We got company."

"You did it the other day."

"Do it yourself."

"I don't have any thumbs. I don't have any goddamn thumbs. Now jack me off, you piece of shit."

"Is that the way we talk to Daddy?"

"Please. Please jack me off, you piece of shit. I don't
have any goddamn thumbs."

'll tell you a little bit more about the demise of my relationship with the woman from the wealthy family. There was that one thing where I had sex with that girl in Columbus, but that wasn't the underlying problem.

The big problem was, we lived in a house, and it had a thermostat. That's it!

'Cause I liked the temperature of the house between seventy and seventy-five, and she liked the temperature of the house between seventy-five and a-hundred-and-fucking-ten. And you can't keep tater salad at that temperature.

We fought about it. She was psycho. Psycho women love me.

We have an argument one night about the temperature of the dwelling. She goes outside with a butcher knife and cuts the tires on my truck.

So I drug up an old Polaroid and entered her in *Hustler*'s "Beaver Hunt." And she won. And I used the money to get me some new tires.

And she superglued my dick to my stomach. So you see how things just get out of hand?

Still itches.

After three years of being married to this woman, I still didn't understand her. She would get mad at me when I was trying to help her.

I'll give you an example. Let's say she'd wake up in the morning and be real bitchy. Let's just say.

And I knew in my heart she was suffering from PMS. And out of my love for her, I would offer her a Midol. And tell her, "Honey, I believe if you eat this Midol, you won't bitch quite so much."

She would growl at me and wouldn't eat the Midol. I had to hide it in a piece of cheese.

I was having an argument about Osama bin Laden with somebody one day. And the argument came up because this country said that if they caught him, they wouldn't extradite him to a state in the United States that had the death penalty.

I'm like, "I don't care." And my buddy's all bent out of shape about it: "I'll blow the towel off his head."

'Cause that's who I hang out with. It bent him out of shape that I wasn't upset about it. He goes, "How come you ain't upset? I know you're pro–death penalty. How come that don't make you mad?"

"You know, I'll tell you why it doesn't make me mad. Because spiritually, Osama bin Laden is prepared to die for Islam. But I guarantee you: Spiritually, Osama bin Laden is ill-prepared to lick jelly out of Thunder Dick's butt crack."

*"I hate grape jelly."*

*"Shut up and lick my butt! And you got to do a good job too, 'cause you're in this till Thunder Dick comes. It ain't just a 'Nah, nah, there I did it.' Boy, you gotta try. You gotta tickle the inside of Thunder Dick's thigh. You gotta fondle Thunder Dick's nut sack a little bit. 'Cause if you don't make him come pretty quick, you're gonna run out of jelly."*

Comedy is not always pretty, folks. Every once in a while somebody will get tongue-fucked in the ass right in the middle of a humorous situation.

I really enjoy performing at the Indian casinos that are popping up around the country. They're all really nice places; the people from all the tribes are great.

I was performing at this new Indian casino up near the Canadian border. And they picked me up in a Mini Cooper. I'm like, "Where am I supposed to sit?"

This guy's defending this car like it's the greatest thing ever made. He's like, "Oh, *no*, *no*, this is made by BMW. It's a great car. You'll see."

We go outside. His battery's dead.

So I give him a jump off my iPod, which is considerably more powerful, it turns out.

I wound up having a great time there and I'm looking forward to going back. But some of these new Indian casinos I know are bogus. Like I was in northern California, performing for the Benihana tribe. I was like, "You know what? Bullshit."

I met the chief. He was the Indian from the Village People.

Just because you have a feather doesn't mean you can open up a casino.


I was at another Indian casino in Hollywood, Florida, in the fall. I performed at the Hard Rock Casino on the Seminole Reservation. And at seventy years old, my mother is my biggest fan, and I called her and I told her where I was. And I hear my father in the background going, "What'd he say?"

And my mother said, "He said in Hollywood, you need reservations to get a cinnamon roll."

"What, Mother?"

"That's what you said."

"You're right."

I lost my ass at that casino. I'll give you some idea how my luck went. The last night I was there, I put a dollar in a soda machine, and nothing came out.

I didn't even get pissed. I just moved on to the next machine, put a dollar in it.

A drink came out, and I was there till dawn. I won four and a half cases of Diet 7-Up.

At a lot of casinos now, they have all these penny slots. How pathetic, you know?

The only thing more pathetic than playing penny slots is watching somebody play penny slots.

"You won a nickel."

But different strokes for different folks, you know? One night I saw a whole family playing penny slots, and they were having a lot of fun. Laughing and giggling.

And the littlest kid won a bunch of pennies. And he shared them with his older brothers and sisters. You know how little kids just spontaneously share?

"They took my pennies, Mommy!"

"Did they get them all? No? Let me have those! Hey, look at all the pennies the brat had."

"WAAH!!!!"

And it got me thinking on a new slogan for the casino industry:

"The family that slots together, stays together."

Bet on it.

I'll tell you how I lost my ass at the Indian casino. The trouble was, I started watching those Texas Hold 'Em tournaments on television. I mean, I'm watching those tournaments like a four-year-old watching the Road Runner.

And the only thing that's dangerous about doing that is that if you watch those shows long enough, you start to think you can play that game for real. But you go into one of those big poker rooms, you find out really quick that they don't let you see everybody else's cards.

I'm sitting there going, "How am I supposed to know how much to bet?"

That Indian casino was beating my ass like a tom-tom at the poker table.

I love westerns, you know. But if they made a western that was set today, to be accurate, instead of the Indians surrounding the settlers and shooting burning arrows at the covered wagons, they'd be saying, "How about a friendly little game of poker, Paleface? See that smoke signal? That's where our new casino is.

"No money? No problem. We'll stake you a stack of chips on the wagon."

That little tour in Florida, our second stop was in Fort Myers. My wife and I wanted to go nearby there to Sanibel and Captiva Islands. That's basically where Jimmy Buffett lived when he was making "Margaritaville." A very, very cool place—very romantic.

The only way to get there is across this rickety little wooden toll bridge. And the toll to cross this bridge is six bucks.

To cross a little rickety fucking bridge. I expected there to be a troll and some billy goats or something.

And I make a lot of money. Not doing comedy. I sell shrimp out of a van.

But six bucks seems like a lot of money. And then when you get up to the little cage where you pay the toll, I swear to God it's true, there's a little sign that says, "No coins or cash."

What do they want you to give 'em, a hand job?

"Buddy, if you just raise that gate a little bit, I'll get my family through. Could you please think of something naughty? My hand is getting tired. I'm only gonna do this for another thirty minutes, and then we're just going to go over to another beach."

When I'm touring, my wife and I usually travel on a big tour bus with our three dogs. We have two Scottish terriers, because if you drink enough Johnnie Walker products, eventually they just send you the dogs. And I qualified early last year.

Their names are Birdie and Bogey. People say, "That's cute. They're named after your golf game."

I'm like, "If they were named after my golf game, they'd be Double Bogey and Where the Fuck Is That Ball Going?" Which is a kind of a long name for a pet.

"Come here, Where the Fuck Is That Ball Going? Go get the ball, Where the Fuck Is That Ball Going? Where the fuck did that ball go, Where the Fuck Is That . . ."

Then there's my English bulldog, Sluggo. He ran away last year, and he was gone for ten hours. All day.

When he came home, just to piss him off, I took him for a walk.

I was in my backyard one day picking up dog shit. And I realized I now have four people working for me full time. And I'm wondering, "How did I wind up picking up the dog shit?"

So now I'm picking up dog shit and reevaluating everybody else's responsibility. And I notice a particularly huge piece of shit. Seriously.

I know it's Sluggo's. 'Cause he outshits the Scotties two to one.

And I'm looking at this pile of shit, admiring it, really. As only a man who picks up a lot of shit can admire a pile of shit. After a while, I start to think it says something on the side of it.

So I go in the house, and I get my glasses. 'Cause I can't read shit without my glasses. . . .

I get back outside with my glasses, and I examine this turd carefully. And I can just make out these words in raised letters: MIDLAND PARK GOLF COURSE. It's a golf glove that Sluggo has eaten, and shat, whole. Velcro and all.

I rinsed it off, and I've been playing with it for two weeks. Is that wrong?

I have never in my life shat a whole golf glove. I shat a rubber glove one time. It said JOHNS HOPKINS on it.

On that tour in Florida I mentioned earlier, we stayed at the Don CeSar hotel in St. Petersburg. It's this great old hotel, built in the 1920s.

We always look for pet-friendly hotels. And the Don CeSar is like overly pet friendly—ridiculously pet friendly. They have a pet concierge that'll come to your room and tell you the services they can offer your pet.

They said, "You can give your pet a massage while you're here."

I'm like, "Oh, sure. I'll buy Sluggo a massage. But I'm gonna tell you right now, he's gonna want a happy ending. This dog loves to get jacked off."

They said they had aromatherapy for pets. I'm like, "What are you gonna make it smell like, ass? That's what he likes. Do you have an ass candle for him?"

*Give your home the fresh smell of ass, with your new ass candle.*

We played the Foxwoods Casino last January in Connecticut. That's the biggest casino in the world. Or it was then.

The people at the Foxwoods Casino were nice enough to let us park our tour bus in a remote parking lot. We're gonna live on the bus while we're there, and we don't want to be too close to all the coming and going at the casino.

Now, the way they came up with the designation "remote parking lot" is this parking lot is nowhere remotely fucking near the biggest casino in the world. Couldn't even see the place from there, right?

The Northeast gets slammed with the biggest snowstorm they've had in ten years. But I've still gotta walk the dogs in the morning. And there's a thermometer on the bus that says what the temperature is outside the bus. And it was zero. And my wife hollers out from the back of the bus, "What's the temperature outside?"

And I said, "There's not one. This place doesn't seem to have a temperature."

No matter what the temperature is, I still gotta walk the dogs, because my wife ain't gonna do it. Not the empress. No, no, no.

So I'm walking the dogs, right? And they pee, right? Which makes me want to pee. It's freezing outside.

My dick is like this:

And normally it's like this:

Huge cock.

It's not long, but it's big around, like a cheese wheel.

"I may not touch bottom, but I will stretch out the edges, with my *cheeeese* wheel. Don't be afraid."

Right after that I went to Fairbanks, Alaska. And my manager's prediction that there wouldn't be a lot of snow in Fairbanks in February was off by about seven and a half fucking feet.

I was stranded in Fairbanks, Alaska, folks, for three days. Count 'em: One, tick ... tock ... tick ... THE FUCK TOCK. Stranded there with the Eskimo people. Not a great-looking group of folks.

And I mentioned that onstage, and they got pissed off. And I didn't see why they got so mad. I didn't insinuate that they had no character. I mentioned that they weren't attractive. I thought they knew. Turns out I let some big cat out of the bag.

Have you seen their teeth? They could make keys.

Anyway, I got this scathing letter from the head Eskimo, Frosty or whatever the fuck his name was. Like halfway through the letter, it said that he would have me know, that the Eskimo tribe was one of the purest races on the planet.

And I was like, that's kind of what I'm talking about. Nobody will fuck these people.

And then later in the letter it said that there were less and less Eskimos every year. So I guess it's getting to where they won't even fuck each other.

Did you hear about the bear they killed up in Alaska? You can see it on the Internet. It was the biggest bear ever recorded in the history of—records.

This grizzly bear was so big, that when it stood on its hind legs it was fourteen feet tall. It could walk up to the average single-story house and look over the top of it.

Now, the bear was killed by a forest ranger, who was out there doing his forest ranger stuff. And then this big grizzly bear charges him, and he's got a 7 mm magnum pistol. He unloads it on the bear, shoots him seven times. And the bear keeps coming.

You know there's a stain developing somewhere, I guarantee you. But this forest ranger reloads and shoots the bear seven more times, kills it. This guy's got balls to the max.

I would have crumpled like a cheap suit. I'd a been laying there praying the bear just wanted to fuck me.

*I wonder if it likes blow jobs.* "Hello, Mr. Bear."

And then I'd shit in my pants just to ruin his meal.

That ain't even the half of it. They're gonna stuff this thing and put it on display in the Anchorage airport. As just kind of a warning to tourists: "Don't go wandering off into the fucking woods, idiot."

So they're examining this bear, and they find five slugs from a .38 pistol in his chest. Then they open up the bear, and they find the gun and the guy who shot it. I shit you not.

Even I know better than to walk into a grizzly bear forest with a .38. What are you going to do, scare a bear with a .38? The bear doesn't know what a fucking gun is.

You can wear handguns in Alaska. We were in a bar, and a guy comes in with a .38 strapped to his side.

I asked, "What are you gonna do with that gun?"

He said, "I'm gonna hunt bear."

I said, "You know what? Here's a little trick. File the sight off the front of the gun."

He said, "Why? So it doesn't affect my aim if the bear gets too close?"

I said, "No, so you don't chip your tooth when you stick it in your mouth to commit suicide, rather than be torn limb from limb while you're still alive to feel it."

And then they were blaming the bear. They said he was a bad bear. He wasn't a bad bear. He was a really old bear. He's tired. But he's smart. He's looking at a deer running 35 miles an hour, and he's looking at a hiker wearing headphones listening to Fleetwood Mac.

The bear's like, "I think I'll have the hiker buffet."

The most dangerous bear of all is the polar bear, did you know that? That's the most dangerous game animal in the world.

More people are killed in zoos by polar bears than by any other animal in the history of—animals. And you can blame Coca-fucking-Cola commercials for that.

"Let's make the most dangerous animal on the planet look like it needs a hug."

I'm on a diet right now, so my life's not worth livin'. Don't you hate that shit?

I'm getting dieting tips from skinny people. That's fun. My mother weighs eighty pounds. Here's her tip: "Drink lots of water. You'll be less hungry."

You know what happens if you drink a lot of water?

You're less thirsty. Just as I suspected.

I still look OK sometimes. 'Cause I wear expensive suits now, and if you drape $5,000 worth of clothes over a pile of shit, it looks all right.

Look bad naked, though. Ain't no hidin' that.

The only person that knows what I look like naked right now, which is the worst I've ever looked, is my wife. And she *has* to have sex with me.

And she makes me wear the suit.

I cut a little hole right here the size of a cheese wheel. And I come in low under the radar.

I was having lunch with a buddy of mine, and my wife. And I was listening to somebody else's conversation, which I know is not a great quality, but it is one of mine.

And it's just kind of a pet peeve. I hate the analogy I heard this guy use. This guy's talking to a friend of his, and he goes, "I have a good job, but I have my cross to bear. The guy I work with talks all day long."

And I'm like, " 'Cross to bear'? That's the analogy you've chosen?"

Folks, do you think at any point while Jesus was dragging this thousand-pound hunk of lumber through the streets of Jerusalem, he ever once said, "Man, this thing is heavy, but at least I don't work with some chatterbox."

I took six weeks off last summer. And then I realized, "I only work three hours a week. What the fuck am I taking a break from?"

Actually, I hurt my knee, and I was laid up for six weeks. I couldn't walk on it. I was just laying around watching TV. And I don't really watch TV much normally.

Anyway, I'm watching these daytime talk shows. There's like five of these shows. And I can't understand how they all stay on the air.

Where do they get the fodder to fuel all these shows, an hour a day, five days a week, fifty-two weeks a year? Are they going around to trailer parks all over America asking people, "Do you fuck your sister?"

"Yeah."

"Get in the truck. Montel, we have a sister fucker."

I was watching an episode of *Montel*. And the theme of the show was male transsexuals who were single-handedly raising their children.

Now, the fact that they found six of these concerns me. I thought there'd be one, right?

No, they got a whole row of these cats, in taffeta ball gowns and bouffant hairdos. Kids in tow.

And I couldn't help but wonder, what kind of stunt did these kids' mothers pull, that would make a judge look at her, and look at "her," and go, "You in the hot pants and the go-go boots, you get the younguns."

These are transsexuals, not transvestites. A transvestite is a man that wears women's clothing. It's perfectly harmless. We all do it.

And actually if a woman wears a man's clothes, that's also being a transvestite, but nobody gives a shit. A woman can put on a man's suit and take out the trash, and nobody cares. But you let the neighborhood watch catch me mowing the lawn in my teddy one fuckin' time, all of a sudden I'm the neighborhood freak.

A transsexual has taken this a step further. A transsexual has taken off the bat pole, and put in a bat cave. For whatever reason.

And the main guy that they were talking to was from Texas—the guy's like six foot three. I just can't imagine a big ole Texan sauntering into a clinic and going, "Doc, I got an idea. What I want you to do is cut off my dick and balls and build me a nice vagina right down there."

You better make sure that's what you wanna do before you do it. Or you'll come back on Monday: "Doc, do you have my dick in a jar somewhere? I regret that whole decision, and I quit drinking tequila."

"Yeah, we do. And we can thumbtack it to your forehead. Now you're a dickhead."

They turned the microphone over to the audience. And they were trying to ask questions that seemed sensitive and pertinent, you know. They're asking questions like, "Was there a point in your life where society failed you, and failed to provide the things that you needed emotionally?"

And I'm like, "Shut up. Somebody ask the real question: What the fuck is wrong with you? You cut your dick off, man."

I wonder if they do keep their dick in a jar. If you do, you run the risk of your kid finding it and taking it to school for show and tell.

"This is my mother's old cock."

Be really funny if the high school bully stopped him on the way to school and said, "I want your lunch. Umm, that needs mustard."

I was at a party the other day, and, this is kind of weird, but I was talking to a friend of mine that I hadn't seen in a while, and a guy comes up to us that he knows, that I don't know. And while we're having a conversation, he stops and introduces me to this fella.

And I'm not paying attention, which I'm usually not. And I go to shake the guy's hand, and while I'm shaking his hand, I realize that it's not really a hand so much as, as, um . . . It's got, like, two pieces of bone with, like, a web or something that goes between them, and then nothing, and then, like, a little stump with a web.

It's a flipper.

Now, no offense if you have a flipper, but if you do, don't you feel some obligation to warn somebody? Especially if you know they're not paying attention. Anything, like, "Watch out, it's a flipper."

Because I ended up accidentally hurting the guy's feelings, you know. I'm like, "Nice to meet you. Wha?! What is that, a fuckin' flipper?"

You feel bad. I'll touch his flipper, I just gotta see it first. Then I'll two-hand it to prove I'm not afraid.

"I'll shake hands with you, Flipper Man. I bet you can really swim fast."

I watched the Michael Jackson trial. And I'll tell you what, Michael wasn't convicted of anything, and I know for a fact that people try to scam rich people out of money.

But here's a little parenting tip, whether Michael is convicted or not convicted, don't let your kid go over to Michael fuckin' Jackson's house. How about that? You know, take responsibility as a parent.

He's got a Ferris wheel in his front yard. I guarantee you, every pervert in America is sitting outside of a school in a hot van with Milk Duds melting in their lap, going, "If I only had a Ferris wheel in my front yard, they'd be lined up at the gate."

I can't imagine as an eight-year-old, my parents sitting me down going, "You're gonna spend a couple of days over at Perry Como's house.

"Some other kids have been over there, and well, things haven't gone so great. But it doesn't hurt much. And we're broke."

I don't know. You hate to judge. But they searched Michael's bedroom, and they found life-size dolls of little boys, one of them dressed in a Cub Scout suit.

Now, maybe it's innocent, but if they searched my bedroom and found a life-size doll of a woman, everybody would assume I was fuckin' it.

And they'd be right.

Before I went back out on the road after I rehabbed my knee, I was doing a few small comedy clubs to warm up before doing big theaters. And I did a show at this little 250-seat club in Atlanta.

The crowd didn't know I was gonna be there. And when I walked out onstage, I saw this big bachelorette party down front, that I didn't know was gonna be there. And if you're a monologist, if you just talk for a living, a bachelorette party is never good news.

Because they're a self-contained entertainment entity. They don't need you. You're just floating out there on their periphery.

Now, I love women. And I especially love drunk women. I always have. But you can't compete with a bachelorette party for attention, because they've got novelty items.

They've got their own little straws, and the top of the straw is shaped like a little penis. *Sip-sip-sip.* And they've got pacifiers, and the pacifiers are shaped like a little penis. *Suck-suck-suck.*

And as the night went on, these ladies laughed harder and harder. Not at me, but at themselves. Because apparently the drunker women get, the funnier they find little tiny penises to be. Which I guess is why I like 'em so much.

Well, in twenty years of doing comedy shows I've

seen a million bachelorette parties. But these ladies had something I'd never seen before. These ladies had an eight-inch-long chocolate penis on a stick, and it was wrapped in cellophane, and nobody was touching it. It was just sitting there in the middle of the table.

And try as I might to ignore it, I could not. Because instinctively I knew that before the night was over, this big chocolate dick was gonna hurt me.

And I was right.

It's a great show, I've got about five minutes left, and for some reason, these girls decide to get this thing out. And they start passing it back and forth to see how much of it they can get in their mouth at one time.

*Nobody* is watching me anymore. Everybody is watching this dunk contest.

And the thing that struck me as odd is that nobody was offended by it. All the women are watching them going, "Oh, aren't they having fun! Don't you remember when Becky had her bachelorette party, and how much fun we had, and where we went, and how much we drank, yakkety-yakkety-yak?"

All the men are going, "Is this free?"

And it's a double standard, folks. Because I guarantee you, if a group of men had whipped out a little sack of gummipussies, everyone would get bent out of shape.

"Slurp, slurp, slurp!" Or however you do it.

I only tell that story because I love to say gummipussy. It's one word by the way. If you say it as two words, it's something else entirely.

# 5

# BACKSTAGE:
## BANNED ON THE ROAD

In the early 1990s, there was a small stretch of my career where my behavior seemed, to some club owners, irresponsible.

I was performing in Columbus, Ohio, at this club I'd played many times. They loved me there. The audiences loved me, and the staff loved me. I was a popular fucking guy. The staff are all younger than me, and I party like a dog with them. When they know I'm coming to town, everybody naps beforehand to rest up and be ready.

Now, in all the times I've performed at this club, I've never had sex with any of the women there. Sunday night comes around, and I'm having fun. I'm at the bar, and I'm doing purple shots, green shots, red shots, clear shots, whatever—I'm taking all comers.

Well, there's this girl there. Let's call her Kathy, just for the purposes of this story; I don't want to hurt anyone's feelings. She's really cute. I'd seen her at this club every time I came to town for years, and she had recently become the girlfriend of the manager, a guy I really liked. Let's say his name was Greg. It was kind of unspoken, but people knew they were dating.

Greg's not there. Kathy's coming up to me and rubbing my leg and whispering to me, and I'm thinking, "This wild woman is hittin' on me."

The club had a little side room where they had music, and this James Taylor–sounding guy was playing there that night. He sounded great, the place was rockin'. And Kathy goes to request a song, and then she comes back and says, "I dedicated this to you, 'cause I've always thought you were hot."

One flirtatious remark leads to another. Just like one drink is leading to another. And we end up going into the women's bathroom and making out up against the wall. She's telling me she wants me to take her home.

We walk out of the women's bathroom. Guess who's standing right there?

Greg. He's just come in.

I know it looks bad. So I don't even say anything. 'Cause I can't think of anything to say.

*I've just been enjoying a taste of your girlfriend at her invitation, Greg, and seriously, man, my compliments. She's really hot.*

I don't think so.

Well, nobody really says anything. We just kind of nod at each other, and I head on back to the bar. And I start talking to one of the waitresses, a girl named

Alison. She has long black hair and she's as cute as she could be, and I've also known her for years because of performing at this club. And I know for a fact that she hasn't had a steady boyfriend for quite a while.

That night she's drinking a little at the end of her shift. I'm still drinking.

And Alison goes, "Why don't we go back to my place and watch TV?"

I'm like, "All right! You're goddamned right we'll go watch TV." I'm sloshed.

We get back to this duplex apartment she shares with another girl. And I go upstairs to her bedroom, I take off my clothes, and I get in bed.

I'm laying there waiting for this little treat to come get in the bed. She's sitting on the couch downstairs talking to her mother on the telephone.

I'm laying on the bed thinking, "She better get up here quick, cause I'm gonna pass out. Fuck it, I'm gonna go get her."

So I walk down the stairs naked. I probably weighed twenty pounds more than I do now, and I've got a hard-on. I say, "Hey."

She looks up and screams like I've got a chain saw and a hockey mask.

Apparently, she wanted to watch television. It wasn't code for anything.

So then she says, "You're going back to the club. Get dressed."

I say, "Oh, wait, I'll be cool." I'm still thinking I can fuck her. But I get dressed, and we go back to the club.

Right next door to the club there was an Italian restaurant with a bar that stayed open late. Alison drops me off at the club, and I go over to the restaurant bar, and there's the rest of the club staff having a few drinks before their day off Monday.

Everybody's there except for Kathy and Greg, and I figure they're off somewhere arguin' or makin' up. I'm hoping it's the latter.

And I'm like, "I'm still in this game." 'Cause there's another cute waitress from the club there, and I take her home. And I do get to have sex with her.

The next morning I'm going to the airport. Guess who's driving me? Greg. And we have the most awkward ride. Finally Greg says, "Kathy said you kissed her in the bathroom."

I feel horrible, because I like Greg and I've known him longer than I've known Kathy. And I don't know exactly what Kathy has said.

So I say, "Yeah, I kissed her."

"You mean you just gave her a smooch? Or did you mash her up against the wall, stick your tongue down her throat, and put your hand in her pants?"

I'm like, well, she told him everything. She just fessed up our whole little sordid affair and put it all on me.

Greg was about to move with her to Portland. So I said, "OK, Greg, here's the deal. We were both drunk, she was hitting on me—"

"That's not what she said!"

"No, I'm sure it's not."

The next day at the club, there are four people who have similar stories to tell, and they're all about the same person: me. Kathy tells her story about me hitting on her in the bathroom, what a skunk. Greg, about me hitting on her in the bathroom, what a skunk. Alison, about me coming down the stairs naked with a hard-on, what a skunk. And the waitress I did fuck is saying, "I was third? What a skunk!" She's madder than the rest of them put together.

Not that I blame her. Finding out you're third choice is flat offensive.

Now, in Atlanta at one time there were three clubs called the Punchline, all owned by the same people. They had a number of Punchline Comedy Clubs throughout the South and Midwest.

I was working the Underground Atlanta Punchline, during the same stretch of my career, and I was throwing too many substances into my body. But I was still doing the job. That's the thing about stand-up comedy. Since you're only working forty-five minutes to an hour a night, you can get into almost any amount of shit and still have time to recover to perform. Until you run into a stone wall with that behavior, and you either change it or it changes you—permanently.

One of the too many substances was acid. They didn't have a Sunday show at the Atlanta Punchline. And on Saturday night, when I was gonna do my last two shows of the week, I had two hits of blotter acid in my pocket that I had bought in Alabama.

That same weekend, friends of mine were performing at the Sandy Springs Punchline, at the Comic Cafe up in Marietta, and at the Improv in Buckhead. And we all make plans to party together on Saturday night at this condo in Buckhead where the Improv put up its performers. The place was right off Atlanta's MARTA rail system, which connects Sandy Springs, Marietta, and downtown. So everyone can get to and from the party safely.

Now this really good friend of several of us—let's call him Bob Hill—was going to be there. And Bob was always a good connection for whatever. Bob was going to get everybody else their acid. And I had the two hits of blotter acid that I bought in Alabama.

We synchronize our watches and agree that after the second show, we'll all eat the acid at the same time and then meet at the condo in Buckhead and trip together all night. I don't have a show the next day, so I feel free to hoot, hoot, hoot.

The Underground Punchline was in a beautiful Victorian 350-seat theater. If it was full, you could really beat it up. It didn't seat a small crowd well, but it sat 350 well. Both my Saturday shows were sold out.

After the first show I start thinking, "They're all gonna be getting their acid from Bob Hill, who always gets the best acid. I got blotter acid from Ala-fucking-bama. I bet my shit is bunk. No great acid comes out of Alabama."

So I eat both hits right then, put 'em under my tongue, two hits, all I've got.

Apparently this acid wasn't made in Alabama. Apparently it was made in a very high-tech lab in California and shipped across the country. And some of it landed in Alabama.

And some of it landed under my tongue between shows on a Saturday night at the Underground Punchline in Atlanta, Georgia.

Twenty minutes later I'm in the green room on my

back with the lights out, going "Uh-oh." I realize I've made a serious judgment error. I should have thought to myself, "Maybe it's great acid, and you shouldn't eat it right before a show. Maybe it's not a good idea to take it beforehand, because you haven't tried it yet and you don't know what it's like." Not looking before I leap again, just like when I was a kid.

I know I'm gonna feel way worse before I feel better. I know I'm on the front end of a twelve- to fifteen-hour ride. Because I'm shocked it's hitting me so fast.

I'm laying there. I hear the show start. I think, "There's no way I can do the show." I'm just spinning. It's just ugly. It hadn't even become fun yet.

The middle act had a didgeridoo, if you can believe it, that he blew onstage. You know, one of those long Australian aborigine instruments sounds like a foghorn blowing underwater?

I'm laying there and I hear that *waaahhh* vibration and feel it going right through my core. I hated that when I was sober, I thought it was a stupid thing, the guy didn't make anything funny of it, he just played it.

I hated it even more now. 'Cause it's the end of the guy's act, and I can hear 'em start looking for me.

When I heard the didgeridoo, I knew my time was coming near.

Finally somebody looks in the green room and

finds me laying there in the dark and turns the light on: "What's wrong with you?"

I said, "I don't feel good." That was my only possible defense. Because I looked like I didn't feel well, and I didn't feel well. I felt like I had made a poor decision earlier.

"Well, you gotta do this show. It's sold out. We got 350 people out here waiting to see you."

I'm like, "Oh, fuck." I had tripped onstage before. But I would do mushrooms, or I would take acid that I knew what it was like. Or I would eat it in the middle of the show as a joke to my friends and get off later. Taking it in between shows was a mistake of a whole 'nother magnitude.

They lead me out to the stage. I think to myself, "Just stick to the show, Ron."

The one thing I've got going for me is that my act has been clicking lately, I've been working a lot, and I'm sharp, I'm in good practice. I do the first punch line perfectly. Boom, a big laugh. I do the next one. Boom, a bigger laugh.

Then I start grinning. I think, "Fuck, I'm gonna beat these people to shreds." I do the next punch line. Boom, another huge laugh.

I can see the rhythm of the material. I'm flowing

with it. Boom, boom, boom. Just that set you get every once in a while when you're just snottin' the room. The set was so good that the staff started to watch. "Fuck, Ron's on fire tonight."

It's the perfect combination of a comic who's done a lot of shows, he's on the top of his game, and it's a great crowd on Saturday night. I'm just doing whatever I want to, bang, bang, bang. I'm having a ball.

Remember, I'm up on a big stage in a theater with a sixty-foot ceiling. It's not like I'm right up close to the audience in a club. So the people can't tell that I'm pale, that my eyes are pinned and my zits are real pronounced. Because they're not focused in on that, they're seeing me as a whole.

I run out of beer, so the staff brings me a fresh beer. For some reason I say, "Look at that. I make you laugh, they give me beer. Later, if I make you jump through a hoop, they're gonna give me a bunch of blow."

Nobody laughs. And in the back, one of the busboys drops a load of dishes. I'm like, "What'd I say?" Now people start looking at my face with suspicion, and they see that I'm fucked up out of my gourd or I wouldn't have said anything that stupid.

I still have twenty minutes left. For the next twenty

minutes, I was like Gene Wilder in *Young Frankenstein* trying to put out the fire, and nobody's buying it.

Now it's Saturday night. I got no Sunday show. So I gotta get paid. The manager of the club, I'd known him for years. I go to his office and he says, "You were a little fucked up onstage tonight, huh, Ron?"

I said, "I'll take a check." I had no story for him, and I saw no need to wait around for cash. But they still owed me money. People paid to get in; I did the show.

I leave, get on MARTA, and go over to Buckhead. The other guys didn't get their acid. Bob Hill, the great connection, didn't come through. They're not sober as judges or anything. They've been drinking.

But I'm tripping my balls off, and I'd bought balloons on the way. I'm blowing them up and batting them against the wall and popping them, and they're trying to watch sports. Their drunk is no match for my acid trip, and eventually they want to go to bed.

They start giving me drugs to try to bring me down, 'cause I'm making so much noise. They're giving me Quaaludes and Valium and Xanax, and nothing's having any effect, I'm still behaving like an ape.

MARTA doesn't run in the middle of the night, so I couldn't leave until it was light. But I had this nice hotel room in downtown Atlanta to go to. So come sunrise, I walk up the hill to get the bus to MARTA.

All the pills start hitting me. I'm like a rhino that's been shot in the ass with a tranquilizer dart. I start going, "Oh, no, what the fuck is happening to me?"

I stumble to the bus stop, and some people help me on the bus. I get to the MARTA station and some people, maybe the same people, help me on a train. And I pass out. I've got a fever blister that's broken and started bleeding. I am a mess, a genuine fucking pure D mess.

I'm passed out on the train for hours, riding back and forth across the Atlanta metro area. Naturally no one wants to touch me to wake me up.

Around two thirty in the afternoon I come to, and I don't know where I am. I wonder, "Am I on an airplane?" It was dark, because we were in a tunnel. Eventually I figure out I'm on a train in Atlanta. It must be a MARTA train. "Which way am I going?" I'm going the wrong way. I get off at the next station and go back the right way.

I get to the hotel and in my room, click, safe. I consider it a home run. I don't realize the damage I've left in my wake.

But soon enough I find out I'm banned from the Punchline. In fact, I'm banned from *all* the Punchlines.

There were six of them, and they had been the first clubs to headline me. Not in the main room at first, but in the small rooms, and then in the main room.

Ten years later, Foxworthy called them and said, "You guys gotta let Ron back in the Punchline."

"Do you know what that motherfucker did?"

"It was ten years ago. You gotta give him another chance. He's one of the funniest guys alive. You've got a club in the South, he's a Southern hitter, how could you not have him?"

"We always liked him. But then he fucking asshole-chumped us."

"I know. But as a favor to me, let him back in."

"All right. But he better not fuck us around."

"He won't."

And I didn't. I came back in and did a good job.

# 6

# ONSTAGE:
## SET 3

I had a great year last year. I got married to my wife, Barbara, a wonderful woman.

When I met Barbara, she was Jeff Foxworthy's interior designer. So not only was Jeff very instrumental in my success and my career, he also introduced me to the woman I'm gonna spend the rest of my life with.

Which I think makes us even.

Barbara is my age. A lot of people thought I would marry a really young woman. But you know what? I wanted to marry somebody that I could stand what they had to say. I've been with women that I just wished that they would shut up so bad, I wanted to hit 'em on the shoulder.

And Barbara's brilliant. She's easy to get along with. And in a few years from now, if Barbara's boobs start to sag a little bit, she can go to a titty doctor and have 'em put right back where they used to be.

If her tummy gets a little big, she can have a tummy tuck, if she wants to. If her vision goes bad, they can do Lasik surgery, give her 20/20 vision at any age. If her hearing goes bad, they can put a device in her ear that'll make her hear as good as the day she was born.

But let me tell you something I've learned over the years, folks. You can't fix stupid.

There's not a pill you can take, a class you can go to. Stupid is forever.

My wife and I live in this new house that my fans bought me. Thanks, everybody. It's just a beautiful, gigantic house in Georgia.

Before this house, the most expensive house I ever bought in my life cost $65,000. This one's more.

In addition to the house itself, I paid all this money to have the landscaping done, and the pool done, and this, that, and the other thing done. But I don't know shit about any of these things, 'cause I've never lived in that kind of house before. And all the people working on the house are just fuckin' me for all they can get.

And the landscape guy, he became my best friend. And he does all this landscaping. And charges me money for it. And he gives me the bill, and I'm like, "God, no way. My old house didn't cost this much."

Then all the plants started dying. And now I can't get the guy on the phone. We're not best friends anymore? What? Come on.

And all I want him to do is do what he said he was gonna do, you know? That's what I do. Do what you say you're gonna do. In business or in your life, whatever.

So I finally get this guy on the phone. I say, "These plants are dying."

He goes, "Well, I'll come over and determine which plants are dying."

We're going through the yard picking out these plants that are dead. And there are these two huge trees that you guys bought me. It's September. The forest is abloom. And these two trees haven't had leaf one on them since they put 'em in the ground. And I tell the guy, "Those two trees are dead."

And this is what the guy does. He goes over to one of the trees, and he scratches the trunk of it with his thumb. And then he comes back over to me and he says this, and I quote, "The core of this tree is still alive."

I said, "Let me tell you what I'm looking for in a fuckin' tree. I'm looking for a tree you can tell is alive, even if you don't know a goddamned thing about trees." I don't want to have to tell everybody that comes over to the house, "Those two trees are fine. If you go scratch the trunk with your thumbnail, you will find a vibrant core."

When I first met Barbara, she had a fifteen-year-old Scottish terrier she was trying to squeeze another year out of.

Soon as I saw this dog I was like, "Oh, shit, this dog is about to die." And I don't want to go through the death of this dog with this woman. I just met her, and I'm not that sensitive.

And sure enough, two weeks later, *clunk*, dead. And she is inconsolable. In bed, sobbing.

Now, I've seen people lose it over the death of a pet, right? But this dog lived fifteen years. If you want much more than that out of a pet, you need to get a tortoise or a tree.

Preferably one with a vibrant core.

Well, she's in bed, sobbing, and I don't know what to do. And I call Foxworthy, and I tell him, "Buddy, I'm lost here." And he goes, "Git her another dawg," or however he talks.

I tell her, "Honey, I'll get you another dog." And she just loses it. "I don't want another dog. I never want another dog. I want my Tatee back."

And I was like, wow. And I listened to it for like a week, and then I'm like, "You know what? I'm gonna get her another dog."

I find a place that breeds Scottish terriers not too far from where we live. And I get her in the car, and I tell her where we're going. And at first she's against it, right? "I don't want another dog. I never want another dog."

But we get down there, she sees them all hopping in the window, "Pick me, pick me." And I buy her this little black Scottish terrier puppy. And I give it to her, and folks, it heals her heart. This little puppy heals her broken heart.

Well, two weeks ago, her father passed away, and I'm like, I think I see a way out of this. So I get her in the car, and she doesn't know we're going to the old folks' home, right? And when I tell her, at first she's against it. "I don't want a new daddy, I don't want a new daddy."

But we get down there, she sees them all hopping in the window, "Pick me, pick me."

She wanted a black one. I'm like, "Keep it simple. Nothing wrong with it. Think it through, though."

He acts weird when I walk in the room, but I think it's because he smells my daddy on me.

For our honeymoon, Barbara and I went on a cruise to Santorini, Greece. And the cruise was fine. We fought the whole time.

And I knew we were going to, because she booked the cruise, and then she shows it to me on the calendar, and the cruise is at the end of the month. Guess what else happens at the end of the month over at our house?

I'm looking at the calendar, going, "Oh, great. I'm gonna spend a week in a little, tiny cruise ship room, trying to get Jeannie back in the fucking bottle."

And my wife's the nicest person I ever met. But you get her PMS-ing and a couple glasses of red wine, and she turns into "Let *me* tell *you* something about *you* that *you* don't know."

And I'm not making light of women's periods. That's some serious shit.

If that happened to me one time, I'd be in the hospital. It wouldn't be any of this nonchalant, "Oh, look, I'm spotting."

Fuck that. I'd be running down the road like my hair was on fire, screaming, "My balls are bleeding, my balls are bleeding!"

But it's our honeymoon, man. And when my wife's on her period, she won't have sex with me at all. No way.

Which is bullshit. Because if the roller coaster is broken, they don't shut down the whole amusement park. Because if they did, you'd be standing outside that fence going, "The log ride's working fine. And I've got some coupins."

Anyway, right before we leave to go on this trip, Foxworthy gives me a Viagra. And I tell him, "Buddy, I don't need that."

He says, "Seriously, dude, you take this on your honeymoon night, you will thank me when you get home."

So I'm like, "OK, I'll try it." So I take it one night, and I walk into our little stateroom. She goes, "I'm just not in the mood." And I'm like, "Yeah, me either."

My dick was hard enough to hunt with. I could have chased down an elk and beat it to death with this dick.

"Oh, shit, I broke an antler. I was gonna have this thing mounted. Now I'm gonna mount this thing. Gimme something else to fuck. Hand me that parrot."

And that wasn't even our biggest point of contention. Our biggest point of contention was that she wanted me to lay out by the swimming pool all day long every day.

Now, normally I would have done it, you know? I'd have just laid there in a lounge chair and read a book, just to shut her up. At this point, I'm out of diamonds.

But I didn't want to lay out by the swimming pool all day long every day, because there was a fan of mine out there. And he wanted to talk to me all day long. Every day.

This guy told me his entire life story, against my will. This guy raped my ear. This guy forcibly shoved unwanted information into my ear hole.

No means no.

And I felt sorry for the guy. I mean, the story was that his wife had left him and started sleeping with all his buddies.

I don't know what I'm supposed to say. "Well, I wish I knew you better. I just fucked an elk and a parrot. My self-esteem's in the shitter."

And that wasn't even the guy's worst quality. This guy was about sixty years old, and he was in great shape—he was a marathon runner.

He was a little bitty guy. He was maybe 5'5", 130 pounds. But he's got this great big nose and these great big, huge hands. And this little tiny bathing suit with what looks like a squirrel living in it. I shit you not.

He's not just standing there. He's leaning this thing into me, and bobbing it around a little bit. I guess to make sure I noticed it. But there's people on the other side of the swimming pool going, "Look at the dick on that guy. I wonder what he feeds it."

We make it to Santorini. And Santorini, Greece, is this little tiny island. It's the partial rim of an ancient volcano. And for two thousand years, folks, the only way to get to the top of the rim on the port side of the island was take a donkey up these switchbacks eight hundred feet. Takes forever.

Until five years ago, somebody built a tram that does the same thing in about eighteen seconds. And I was really shocked to see the donkey guy still in business, because he had the worst sales pitch I ever heard in my life.

"You can take the donkey to the top of the rim, or you can take the tram. It is the same price."

That would be my biggest secret if I were you, buddy. I'd start lying to people as soon as they got off the ship.

"The donkey is three-fifty. The tram is around twenty-eight hundred euro."

"Shit, saddle me one up. Come on, honey, it'll be fun. And you're in such a good mood. Maybe a donkey ride would be just the thing to cheer you up."

Well, as it turns out, I'm a tram guy. So we take the tram up, and then we've got to walk up from that, up these ancient cobblestone streets, up, up, up. Because there's one more church in the Mediterranean, we haven't seen it.

And I'm sweating scotch from every pore on my body. There was a huge party the night before, and I was more fucked up than Courtney Love at the Pamela Anderson Roast.

I woke up the next morning, my head felt like I went on a date with Robert Blake.

We're trudging up this mountain. And I know I've got about ten minutes of this left in me, and I'm gonna want to go back to the ship and sleep it off, and that's gonna piss her off even more.

And we walk by this little place that rents scooters. And I tell my wife, "Why don't we rent one of these scooters? We can buzz around the whole little island on a little scooter."

She goes, "We are not getting on one of those scooters."

I said, "Let me rephrase that. I'm gonna rent a scooter. And if you'd like to, at some point, hop on the back of it, that'd be fine. Or you can watch my little tail light fade away into the distance!"

She goes, "You don't even know how to ride a motorcycle!"

I said, "I've been riding motorcycles my whole life!"

As it turns out, though, I don't know how to ride a scooter. This thing was a piece of shit, man. It had a front wheel the size of a doughnut, and my knees are in my ears, my hands are two inches apart on the handlebars, buses are roaring by.

She's screaming, "STOP THIS THING, GODDAMN IT!"

I'm screaming, "LEAN THE WAY I LEAN, GOD-DAMN IT!"

Like a monkey in a sidecar.

After a while we start to get the hang of it. And we make our way down the gentle, sloping other side of Santorini. And you get down there, and it's just these knockout beaches and bars and restaurants.

It's the promised land. My promise. We make up from our little tiff, and we start walking down the beach, hand in hand.

It turns out that part of the beach is a nude beach. Guess who's there?

Squirrel Man.

And he has got what looks like an anaconda laying in his lap. As soon as I saw it I told my wife, "That thing musta ate the squirrel."

And he's not even laying flat on his back. He's leaning toward the people that are walking toward him.

And I didn't begrudge him a bit, because if it would have been mine, I would have been holding a picture frame around it.

"You can take the donkey to the top of the rim, or you can ride this. It is the same price."

The first time my wife and I made love, it was a little awkward, because well, you've heard of these screamers, right?

Well, apparently, she had never been with one. 'Cause I'm going at it, "Ah, ah, ah, ah, ah!" She's like, "What's up with that?"

"I'm a screamer, baby. Daddy makes a little racket in the sack."

I make fun of my wife. But she is just a brilliant woman—two degrees.

She came up with a solution for the overpopulation of our planet. It was a brilliant idea—and simple, like most brilliant ideas are. Stop spending money, she said, on research for the development of products like Viagra and Cialis.

And instead . . . instead . . . invest that money in research to develop a product that'll make semen taste like . . . chocolate.

She'd be chasing me down the sidewalk: "Come here, Willy Wonka! Get that little chocolate factory back over here, mister. There's gotta be one more in there."

Normally my wife's a very sensuous woman. One time we were driving down the road, and she decided to give me the highway delight. Or, as I like to affectionately refer to it, a mouth hug.

And I was pleasantly surprised, but the other people in the carpool got all pissed off.

"We gotta get these kids to school."

"She loves chocolate."

I think it's kind of odd that in twenty years of constant traveling doing stand-up comedy, I've never become a member of the mile-high club. That's where you have sex in a plane over a mile off the ground, or however the hell you got up there.

I did jack off in Denver two weeks ago. And I met John Elway.

Not at the same time.

*Nice to meet you, Mr. Elway. Do you like chocolate?*

I am a member though, oddly enough, of a little club I started, called the mile-ahead club. That's where you fuck someone behind a Cracker Barrel billboard. We're having a membership drive too. So, uh, grab your partner and skip to my Lou.

My wife got her nipples pierced. She didn't ask me nothing about it, you know. She just went ahead and did it.

I'm just not into it. And I think you should ask your mate if they're into that, before you do it. This whole piercing thing just left me sitting on a fucking island, waving bye at all the people sailing off to get pierced.

I just don't get it. I was talking to a girl the other day, and she had a pierced tongue. And I asked her why she did it. And she said, "It helps my boyfriend enjoy oral sex."

And I'm like, "No, it doesn't. You know what helps your boyfriend enjoy oral sex? Oral fuckin' sex. There's no need to decorate it, sweetheart."

I'm telling you, folks, out of all the erections I've ever had in my life, it never occurred to me to rub steel on one of them.

"No, wait a minute, stop, stop, that doesn't feel good. Uh, what I want you to do is get the dull edge of a butter knife, and just rake it up and down the shaft.

"Now set a mousetrap off on my nut sack. Now we're both having fun."

Now, bellybutton piercing, that can be OK. But it's gotta be the right girl, right? That tan girl at the park, with the low-slung faded jeans, little pink half shirt, little silver hoop. That's sexy.

But have you seen these women that pierce their fat roll? Now, I'm not being an ass. I've got a huge gut too. But you're never gonna see me at the mall in a tube top with, like, a horseshoe poking through there.

I own a *mirror*.

My wife got her nipples pierced, though. I just came home one day, you know, she opens up her robe and there it is. And I was, like, "Whuh?"

She goes, "What's the matter?"

"Nothin'."

"Don't you think it looks sexy?"

I said, "It looks like the plug in my grandmother's bathtub."

Don't ever fuckin' say that, guys. I haven't seen them titties in six weeks.

I was playing the Paramount Theatre in Austin, Texas, and Mother lives in a little town outside of Austin, where you guys bought her a new house. She says thanks.

And I was at Mother's house having dinner, and there's eight of us sitting around this big table eating Mother's fried chicken. Great chicken. And Mother is telling a story.

And Mother has had a couple cocktails. Couple. Mama drinks.

And the story was, she had her car worked on. They gave her a loaner car. She brings the loaner car back, there's a big dent in the fender. She has no idea how it got there. I'm sure she's telling the truth.

And I guess what she meant to say was the guy comes out and sees she wrecked the car, and he chews her out because there's a big dent in the fender. But what she says is this:

"And you know what he did? He just ate me out right there in the parking lot in front of everyone. I didn't even do it. He's eating me out right in front of all these people."

I got chicken flying out of my nose. And my slack-jaw dullard family doesn't even get it.

They're like, "That ain't right, he just ate you out like that. You oughta take somebody in private, you gonna eat them out. I've always said that."

I was like, "So he wasn't mad, Ma?"

"Yeah, he's mad. He's eating me out right there in the parking lot in front of everybody. There's five people standing there watching this man just eat me out right there in the parking lot."

I went, "Mama, the expression is *chewed* me out."

"It's the same thing."

"Technically, no, Mom. The next time you tell the story, I would say 'chewed me out.' Especially if you tell it at church."

I think the most often asked question I have on my Web site is why I wasn't a bigger part of *Blue Collar Television*, which is Jeff and Larry and Bill's show.

And the answer is, my work ethic. It's questionable.

My grandpa used to say, "That boy's got a lot of quit in him."

And as a young man, the things I didn't quit, I got kicked out of. I got kicked off the high school debate team for saying, "YEAH, WELL, FUCK YOU!"

I thought I had won. The other kid was speechless. That's what I thought we were trying to do.

And Larry the Cable Guy, speaking of you can't fix stupid, let me tell you what he did. He spends the night at my house.

And don't ever let him spend the night at your house, by the way. Even if it's raining.

He spends the night at my house, and we get into the whisky deep, for no reason. It's a Tuesday night, we're just *glug-glug-glugg*ing away. We wake up the next morning, he gets on his tour bus and goes to who the hell knows where. I wake up with a living, breathing hangover that has its own soul.

I named it Chuck.

And I'm going through this house we just moved into, and I can't find one aspirin in the whole house. My head is exploding. So I gotta get in my car and face the morning sun, which I geared my entire career around not having to do. And I go to the store, and I go in, I buy some Excedrin.

I come back out to the car, and I pop a couple of them in my mouth. And I can't swallow them because my mouth is dry, right? I'm kind of choking on them, you know?

But luckily, in the seat where Larry was the day before, there's a Diet Coke bottle with about two fingers' worth in the bottom of it. And I unscrew the lid, and throw it back.

And slowly my brain starts to process information. Does Diet Coke make a wintergreen pudding product? Sort of a stringy wintergreen pudding?

And then it dawns on me, I'm drinking his fuckin' spit. I'm outside my car licking the grass to get the taste out.

The same thing happened to me later. Not the same thing, really, but the same kind of thing. I was on my way to the airport, and I stopped on the way for some iced tea with a wedge of lemon in it.

And I parked my car at the airport on the top floor of the parking garage, in the sun, and I'm gone for two weeks. I come back, and I get stuck in traffic on the way home. And I'm not even thinking, I just reach over and pick up this two-week-old remains of iced tea with lemon, and I chug-a-lug it down.

And slowly my brain starts to process information. Is that lemon moss? Is that some sort of a citrus algae river product?

And I take the lid off the styrofoam cup, and it's this nasty science experiment. And I open my truck door and throw up in the stalled traffic.

But oddly enough, two weeks later a rash on my nuts clears up. There's your silver lining right there.

I get chastised publicly in the media for my position on the death penalty. To tell you the truth, they don't even know the half of it.

Because in the Scott Peterson case, I'd want to be the guy that sets the execution date. And I'd set it for one a.m. the day they set clocks forward. Just so I could walk in and go, "Well, looks like you got about another hour, Scott. . . .

*"Not.* Spring forward, asshole!"

There is one piece of legislation floating around right now that I endorse publicly, and with all my heart. I believe if you're a convicted sex offender in this country, when you get out of prison, you should have to put a sign in your yard or on your door that says you're a convicted sex offender. Because I don't give a fuck about your rights anymore.

And I'd also like to know where to get those signs, because I'd like to keep some kids out of my yard.

"Don't go in Mr. White's yard, he'll fuck ya. Is that a Ferris wheel?"

I've talked about my cousin Ray before. And there's no two people on the planet that are less alike than he and I.

I'll give you an example. He's a homophobe. And I can't believe I'm not gay. That's how far apart we are on the food chain.

Now, I'm not gay, but if you ever come to see me live, take a look at the fuckin' shoes I wear. The reason I say that is who knows how things are gonna turn out in life?

And the reason I say that is from the time I was nine until I was thirteen, I was raised by my grand-mother. And my grandmother and her family moved to the Panhandle of northwest Texas at the turn of the last century in a covered wagon. Very poor, very rural people.

And as a child, I would just have to look a little bit sick, and my grandmother would start cramming things in my ass.

She had an anal thermometer from the 1800s the size of a rolling pin. And the only way she had to take my temperature was to shove this huge antique glass rod into my butt.

And suppositories—gigantic ass pills. I don't know where she got them. She would take these gigantic pills and shove them in my butt.

And enemas, she would stick a hose in my ass and pump hot water into my bowels. And I hated it.

At first.

Then I was like, "I feel dizzy, Grandma. Was that my fever breaking?"

We were living in a podunk little shit town. And there's nothing to do, right?

Well, the year I lived with her that I turned thirteen, I figured out something really fun to do. And my grandma caught me in the bathroom, just a-doin' it.

And my grandmother, bless her heart, was a very religious woman. And she came up to me later and said, "It says in the Bible, young man, that it is better for your seed to fall in the belly of a whore than on the ground."

I was like, "Well, it's tough to argue with that kind of logic, Grandma. You got fifty bucks?"

My grandmother had some kind of special radar when it came to me and sex. 'Cause the first time I ever had sex in my life, that somebody else was involved in, my grandmother caught me in her garage having sex with this girl.

And my grandmother said, "One of these days you're gonna be standing side by side with the Lord, watching your life pass before your eyes, answering for each and every one of your sins. And what are you gonna say to him, young man, when this little episode turns up?"

And I said, "I'm gonna tell him: 'Watch this, here comes the good part. I was only fifteen, but I was throwing some dick in this one, wasn't I? Look at that right there. That sumbitch could go.' "

I was talking to Cousin Ray one day, and he said, "Man, this world would be better if there weren't so many queers."

And I said, "You know what, the next time you have a thought, let it go. We're all gay, buddy. It's just to what extent are you gay."

He goes, "That's bullshit, man. I ain't gay at all."

I'm like, "Yeah, you are, and I can prove it."

He goes, "Fine. Prove it."

I'm like, "All right, do you like porn?"

He goes, "Yeah, I love porn, you know that."

I'm like, "Oh, do you only watch scenes with two women together?"

He goes, "No, I watch a man and woman making love."

I'm like, "Oh, do you like the guy to have a small half-flaccid penis?"

He goes, "No, I like to see a big hard, throbbing—"

"Do you like chocolate?"

# 7

# BACKSTAGE:
## THE ADVENTURES OF SEÑOR WHITE

The opening shot is from high overhead. We're looking down at a ditch at the side of a dirt road in Mexico.
Zoom in a little, there's somebody lying in the ditch.
Closer. It's me. Passed out, no shoes, empty bottle of
scotch in my hand.

And my voiceover says, "I've always loved Mexico."

That was the first scene of a pilot for a sitcom that
Fox produced in Los Angeles in the winter of 2003. It
was gonna be called *Señor White*. And what it was
about was my real-life experiences running a pottery
business in Reynoso, Mexico, along the border from
McAllen, Texas.

Now, because of its advantageous location, Reynoso was a considerable trans-shipment point for illegal drug traffic. Not that there were many drugs to be
had in Reynoso itself. The cartels didn't want some
petty local action interfering with their pipeline; they
wanted a nice quiet town to run their shipments
through. And if you stayed out of their way, they never
gave you a second thought.

That said, it was also true that "tragic accident"
was a very popular category of death in Reynoso. And
anyone who interfered with the drug trade was a
likely candidate for it.

"Look there, now, isn't that a pity? Five bullets to the back of the head. What a tragic accident."

How I got to be in the pottery business in Reynoso, Mexico, is that I was living with this woman I couldn't stand on Lake Lyndon Baines Johnson, just northwest of Austin, Texas. And she couldn't stand me either, like all the women I was involved with in that part of my life. I'm gonna call her Phyllis, so I can tell you what happened.

Now aside from my relationship, living on Lake LBJ is nirvana, I'm in my fucking heaven. I got a house, not a great house at all, but it's a lake house. It sits right on this cove of Lake LBJ, which is a twenty-two-mile-long lake on the Colorado River that LBJ had dammed up. And he just happened to own three thousand acres right on the side there. So he flooded his neighbors' land, and now he's got beachfront property. That's a lucky coincidence there.

It's good to be the king. You can adjust some shit: "Well, there should be a pond here, I think."

Johnson City is near there, and you can tour LBJ's childhood home if you want. I did, and halfway through the tour when they said his wife's name I went, "Lady-bird. Oh, I thought *Larry* Bird lived here. When I didn't see a basketball hoop outside, I was wondering, *How'd he get so good?*"

Phyllis was kind of an artist-craftsperson—she wasn't making any money. But my career was going pretty good. I was making $1,800 a week and airfare, and that was good, solid headliner money then. And I was banging, I was doing a good job, and I was popular with the club owners.

The relationship has gotten to the point where I can't stand Phyllis and she can't stand me. But at the same time, I'm still wishing that it can work. I'm seeing these glimpses of things in the relationship that are not fixable, but I'm trying not to see them.

She used to say, "I know you think I'm *stupit*."

"No, honey, I don't think you're *stupid*. At all."

But I'm making good money, like I said. And there's not a lot of hassle involved. The Funny Bone at one time owned twenty-one clubs. So the majority of my year I could book with one phone call with the people who ran the Funny Bone clubs. They were my anchor gigs.

But in the early '90s the clubs weren't doing the business they used to do. Some of the audience that got excited about going to comedy clubs in the 1980s, when the comedy club scene really exploded, were parents with kids and they weren't going out anymore like they used to. So the club owners felt that squeeze, and sooner or later so did everybody who worked for 'em.

The Funny Bone management tells me this year it's not gonna be $1,800/week and airfare, it's gonna be $1,500 flat. I told them, "Go eat a bowl of steaming fuck." Which was fun to say, but expensive.

'Cause right about then comedy clubs were closing up all over. It wasn't like I had all these alternative clubs to go play.

So I needed my girlfriend, Phyllis, to get a job. We got a house payment, I got a $500/month payment on my custom van, I got $500/month child-support payment. And I just got my pay cut by a third or more when you figure in what I'm going to have spend on airfare.

Now, I knew this guy who was related to people at Southwest Airlines. So I figured if Phyllis got a job with Southwest, I could fly for free and that would be worth another $1,400/month besides whatever her salary would be. Plus she'd be able to fly to see me on the road.

I get her an application and fill it out with her. For hobbies, I had her put down that she was a middle-distance runner. I thought that'd be kind of unusual and memorable, make her application stick out.

Now, I know she doesn't want to go to work. I know she just wants to stay at home and potter around with her pottery. But we fill out the application, and she promises to send it in. Two months later, we still haven't heard from Southwest.

Now, I know my friends weren't giving me a line. I know they're ready to give her a job. And one day I take out the trash, and stuck to the bottom of the trash can I find the greasy application that she threw away.

Now, not too long before this, she caught me fucking somebody else. There was a note left in my briefcase: "I'll never forget the time we spent together. (signed) Michelle."

It might as well have said, "Ron, you left some of your things in my ass."

I figure Phyllis and I are even, because we lied to each other. I still didn't admit I fucked this girl, which I had a hundred times. She was a girl I knew in Memphis from before I met Phyllis. I figured fucking Michelle was grandfathered in.

Anyhow, Phyllis didn't budge from her original position, which was, "I'm an artist. I have to do my art. That's what's really important to me right now."

"OK, sure, honey, I understand."

And what she was doing was not really being a

potter. She was a mosaicist. She was taking an already-made bowl and doing mosaic tile application to it.

And she was really making pretty stuff—she did have a good eye, and a creative design sense. But it took her forever to make these bowls. She took six months to make four bowls.

She took those four bowls to a weekend craft fair, sold every one the first morning, made $90. Then she took another six months to make four more bowls to take to another craft fair to sell for $90.

She's bringing in $3.75 a week. That's some cash flow there.

The pay cut has made me sick to my stomach. I'm feeling like I've got to find some other way of making a living. And I'm kind of impetuous and don't always think things out. I'm looking at this mosaic tile appliqué pot one day and I say to myself, "What somebody oughta do is go down to Mexico, hire a bunch of women to pop these things out, and have Phyllis orchestrate the designs."

I flashed on this vision of a big old adobe-and-brick building in a little Mexican town. And inside it's got these great big timber posts and beams and rafters. And there are sweating pitchers of lemonade, and women making tortillas and barbecuing a goat.

It's a vision of paradise.

The next day I drove down to Mexico. My ex-sister-in-law was living down in McAllen, Texas, with a Mexican girl, who knew a cop on the other side of the border in Reynoso, Mexico, whose grandfather owned a ranch that had been run for him by a woman named Irma Munoz from the time she was sixteen. Irma ran the whole operation. She not only took the cattle from the field to the slaughterhouse, she also took the meat to market and ran the market.

Irma worked for this man until she was thirty-four. Then he sold all his ranches, except for one, which he gave to her, making her a fairly well-to-do woman until the peso got devalued. She and her husband are doing OK. He's a big strong guy who built their house with his own two hands out of cinderblock. And he's got this cheesy operation bottling motor oil. He's got a big tank and a bunch of plastic bottles that they fill by hand.

They've got these Guatemalan guys working there who have escaped the civil war in Guatemala with machete cuts through their eyelids. They've been through the shit and have come to Reynoso to make the big money. That's their El Norte.

Now, by this time in her life, Irma Munoz is a big old fat lady, who is kind, sweet, smart, and confident.

She's a pillar of the *colonia*. The local women look to her for advice. She and her husband are important figures in the local church community.

I told Irma my vision, I hired her, and she made it happen. Right around the corner was a tortilla factory that had been abandoned before it was ever opened. The fella who built it died in a tragic accident, which like I said was kind of common there.

The place has got no windows. It's been empty for ten years. There's six inches of cat shit everywhere. Nothing works. I look at it and I'm like, "Perfect. This is the place."

Irma found the guy who owned it and arranged for us to rent it for $90/month, if we would do work on it. The next morning I show up with Phyllis, and Irma has hired five women and they're already at work cleaning it up.

Eventually we have eight women working there. We have it all cleaned up. We've run electricity in, we've run plumbing in. I've got an accountant. We're running a legitimate business, Irma's making the money she needs, and we're paying the other women a decent wage. And Phyllis is the design director.

It's just what I pictured. We've got lemonade pitchers sweating in the heat in the workshop. I'm buying goat meat at the corner store. We eat lunch together. Every once in a while the local priest stops by, he blesses the place one day.

I'm doing comedy gigs with Jeff Foxworthy on the weekend, because it turns out I'm not really selling this stuff, I'm collecting it. Everybody is starting to notice, we got a shitload of this stuff piling up.

And the whole time, Phyllis and I are not getting along. It was vicious. She was a good cook, and we had great sex. So you wanted it not to be true.

I found this local golf course called Compestre Golf Course, where I met these great men I played golf with three times a week. One of them had come to Reynoso when he was fourteen, after both his parents died in a tragic accident. He came to Reynoso with a dirty blanket and a sack of biscuits, and put three sons through medical school. And he doesn't even see it as a big achievement.

He started working for a brick factory. There were a lot of brick factories in Reynoso at the time, because Houston was booming and they were sending the bricks up there. Shitty fucking bricks, too, you could cut a hole through 'em with a quarter.

He made $2/week. By the time he was twenty-one, he owned his own brick company. He was the first person in Reynoso to build big old rudimentary clay kilns and start firing his brick. The other brick factories were just making sun-dried adobes in brick size.

At one time there were sixteen brick companies. Now there was one: his.

When I'm on the road with Jeff, I can't wait to get back. I'm having fun, I'm being respected by the *colonia*. It feels wonderful living in this community.

But I don't have the wherewithal to make the whole thing work. I'm creating an illusion. I'm going even more broke than I was before, funding this shit, because I love it.

One problem we had was that putting mosaic tile onto clay pots created a product that was heavy and fragile, which is a bad combination. You want heavy and sturdy, or you can deal with light and fragile. But heavy and fragile sucks. Because you're gonna run into some shipping problems. We found some places in California to take them on consignment, but they're getting there in a million fucking pieces.

Now, if we'd gotten this great packing equipment that I wanted, you could have kicked them to California and they'd be fine. Because you could blow liquid foam around them, and it'd be unbreakable.

I was talking to the brick king about it. He showed interest in it, he thought we made beautiful stuff.

And I just wanted to figure out how to keep my

dream going and keep being part of this community Irma and I had created.

Phyllis didn't have the same feeling. She and the women working for us didn't get along, and she wouldn't take the time to try to communicate with them.

Neither of us spoke a word of Spanish when we got there. But I learned some and spoke to people in Spanish as much as possible. It wasn't good Spanish, but I could communicate a little bit. I also had a college student named Miguel as my interpreter, because I was doing business and I couldn't just guess at things, and that slowed down my learning.

Phyllis couldn't be bothered. I started dreaming about a tragic accident. In my fantasy, an Exxon truck running a stop sign takes her out. She never feels a thing.

The driver's drunk, with a prior record of drunk driving that the company didn't do a background check on. And I'm in court crying over my dead wife. It's a $20 million case.

By now I've got a compound full of this pottery. I'm filling up warehouses, but I'm doing it for love. The part that happened is the part I envisioned. I didn't envision the other part: carrying the shit across the border and driving five hours to San Antonio to put it on consignment, shipping it to California in one piece, and a million other details that you gotta figure out if you're gonna run a successful business.

Phyllis is gaining weight. She won't cook. She won't screw me.

I'm fucking everything I can fuck on the road. My weight's way down. I'm running. I'm taking care of myself.

It's all casual sex, until I run into this old friend on the road, in her hometown. We go out to dinner right across the street from her apartment, and she introduces me to the waitress and says, "Ron is my sexual fantasy."

I'm like, "Oh." 'Cause I never really considered it. I thought we were just good friends. "But now that you mention it."

So she and I go back to her apartment, and we're making out on her bed, and I reach down to push her legs apart, and her leg falls over like a manhole cover that's being held up by a watch spring. Wham. I got my hand down her panties, and then her roommate comes in and says, "What about your boyfriend?"

Then we didn't see each other for a while. Then we're both traveling, we run into each other in Las Vegas, and we almost immediately start making out. We go to her room and we fuck like we both just got out of prison. I rip the fucking headboard off the wall, I'm throwing some dick.

She used to come to the lake house, when she was in Austin, so she knew Phyllis. I start making excuses to meet her different places. I'm lying to Phyllis about going to Austin or wherever for a tryout for the Montreal Comedy Festival or what have you.

Then I go to Denver to see this lady, and I don't even give Phyllis a cover story. So Phyllis decides I'm fucking somebody. And my lady love is leery of everything, because she knows Phyllis is crazy.

One night Phyllis is drunk and she calls the lady I'm fucking to help her figure out what lady I'm fucking. At first, my friend thinks Phyllis knows the truth. Then she realizes Phyllis doesn't know. And in the course of this, Phyllis tells her, "Sometimes when I watch Ron sleep, I just want to kill him."

She decides right then and there, this shit is over, she won't see me, she won't return my calls. Finally she returns my call and she says, "Listen, Ron, I like you a lot. But I can't do this, and here's something you need to know. Phyllis told me that sometimes when you're sleeping, she just wants to kill you."

Foxworthy knows Phyllis is crazy. And he's already

told me, "If you move back north of the border and stop doing all the drugs and shit you're doing in Mexico, I'll put you up in any hotel in America for as long as you want to live there, and I'll pay for it."

Anyway, my friend who was once my lover and is now officially my ex-lover tells me what Phyllis told her, and she says, "But you gotta remember, Phyllis was really drunk when she said that about wanting to kill you."

And I'm like, "That doesn't help. The only time I tell the truth is when I'm drunk. I don't feel any safer because she was drunk when she said it."

So I decide to get out. But it's hard to leave. We have two dogs. We have a nice house across the street from a church in a nice, quiet neighborhood in Reynoso. It's not where the brick king lives, but it's nice.

And I love it there. It's the Wild West. I was born to live in the fucking Wild West.

One day the new police chief was quoted in the paper saying he was going to stop the drug traffic going through town. You've heard of a death wish. Apparently, the new police chief had a tragic accident wish.

My favorite restaurant in the city was La Mansión. It was a very cool-looking place with great big ceilings. A few days later the police chief's having dinner at La Mansión with the district attorney and a third man. The third man stands up and unloads a pistol in the police chief's chest. Another tragic Reynoso accident.

I wasn't eating there at the time. But that became my favorite table.

And you gotta realize that even if my finances aren't as healthy as the brick king's, I'm still in the upper 1 percent income bracket in Reynoso. It's the only place I've ever lived where I could make that claim.

So I could always eat at the best places when I wanted to, like La Mansión. But I ate off the taco stands too. My son used to come down a lot and he loved it. We ate off this great fucking taco stand right across the street from the church right by our house. The locals would congregate there.

It was a high-end taco stand. The proprietor made a better taco and he charged more. And if you bitched about the price, he would tell you where to go to get a cheaper one.

"Is that all you care about is cheap? Then you don't eat at my taco stand." He was the taco Nazi, like the soup Nazi on *Seinfeld*.

He had Cokes in the original bottle on ice. A few of Coca-Cola's Mexican bottlers never abandoned the original bottle. And there's just something about them. They're as great as a Coke ever was.

There was a place in the neighborhood that made carnitas. Every day this man rendered a hog, and he used every part of the pig for something. Like the skin for crackling. Then he would make his deep-fried pork lard, and it was so fucking goddamn delicious. Some of it he sold to restaurants and the rest he sold to the public until it was gone. And there'd be people arguing over the heart and the liver and so on.

He would just put it on a scale and wrap it up in some foil and give that to you with some hard tortillas and this great salsa that his wife made. You didn't know what part of the pig you got until you opened up the foil.

One day Marshall and I took some home. We opened it up, and there was a perfectly round thing with two holes in it—it was the fucking snout. And Marshall said, bless him, "At least it doesn't have one hole."

Meanwhile Phyllis is just a mess. She's not taking care of herself. She hates everybody.

I want out, but I can't just leave her in Mexico. Her family knows she can be impossible, and they're surprised I've put up with her for so long. I call 'em—

I still to this day talk to her family—and I tell 'em, "You gotta come and get her. 'Cause I can't leave her here, but I'm not gonna stay with her either. We gotta have an intervention."

It was a bad scene. Her parents drove down from Omaha pulling a big fucking trailer. And her brother-in-law and sister came down.

Most of the stuff we had in the house was hers. 'Cause just before our relationship began I had gotten divorced from Marshall's mother, and I just walked out of that. I left the house, the furniture, the washer and dryer, I left it all, 'cause I didn't need it, I was gonna be on the road.

I know Phyllis's not gonna take kindly to the intervention. When her parents show up, she won't even let 'em in the house. Finally we make this arrangement where I'm gonna put her on a plane first class, which was a big deal to us. That's a bonus. And I'm gonna pack the stuff, all the household stuff and all the pottery, and get it to her—she's gonna have it all.

The brick king has become an investor and he's just gonna take it in the fucking ass. I'm just gonna give her the shit, and I'm gonna tell him I don't know what. And I know he won't care. Which he didn't. He had written it all off before then. He knew we didn't have a marketing plan and a distribution system and all. He just came over one day and said, "This is cool." He fell in love with it, like I did.

Some of the bigger pieces had a hundred hours of labor in them. The stuff was beautiful, and when people saw it, they loved it.

I had created this whole Mexican craft-artist identity for Phyllis. It was all laid out in this beautiful brochure I had made, how her grandfather was a master mosaicist in Mazatlán who did the churches in Machu Picchu.

I called my buddies Steve Cook and Sam Bartholomew because I had to go on the road, and I said, "Steve, I need you to come down here and I need you to drive a truck out of Mexico."

He said, "You got it. I'll be there tomorrow and I'll help you get packed up and get you out of there."

Phyllis was already gone.

My initial plan had been to say, "I'm leaving, and I'm taking the dogs," hoping it could now be about the two dogs we had.

I was hoping she'd say, "You're not taking the dogs. Those are my dogs."

Then I could say, "OK, you can have the dogs. Bye."

I knew I was gonna do this two weeks before I did it. So I just felt guilty. 'Cause I loved these fucking dogs. They were two great Labs. I'd look at 'em and think, "Oh fuck, I'm sending you off. There's nothing I can do. I'm using you as a fucking tool."

It didn't work worth a shit. She said, "I don't give a fuck about the dogs. You're not gonna leave me. Kill the fucking dogs."

So I also had to find a good home for the dogs, which I fortunately did. And Steve came down from San Antonio to help me pack up and convoy everything to Dallas.

When I drove into Mexico, I had the biggest truck Ryder rents, with the biggest trailer Ryder rents behind it. Then I had my custom GMC van with the biggest trailer Ryder rents behind it. Convoying south on Highway 287.

Four years later I have the exact same equipment heading north on Highway 287, and I went, "Well, that was a bad idea."

Steve and I convoyed to Dallas. My stuff was in the trailer behind the van, and Phyllis's stuff was in the Ryder truck and its trailer. Sammy, my dear friend, drove the Ryder truck and trailer to Omaha, unloaded it all.

Then I started living in Sammy's attic. I thought it was great. I'd been living my life a long fucking time and that amounted to me being broke. I had a mattress on the floor, a crystal peanut bowl the Foxworthys gave me for Christmas, a pillow, and a blanket.

I'm like, "All right, whatever, we start again. We just fucking start again."

I felt great. I still had a career. Foxworthy was making rumblings about this idea he had for a "blue-collar comedy tour." I was hoping for good things.

Three years later, the Blue Collar Comedy Tour was going strong, and Warner Brothers was getting ready to release a concert film in theaters.

Then Fox got interested in *Señor White* and spent $2.2 million making the twenty-two-minute pilot, which was funny as shit. I'm prejudiced, of course, but everybody who saw it liked it.

Great people worked on it. Betty Thomas was the director. She had become a big-time movie director after being part of the cast of *Hill Street Blues*. We had a good cast, and most of the characters were just like the real people in Reynoso. Except that in the show Irma wasn't a big old fat lady, she was a fox with these great fucking titties.

We had a seven-day shoot on the pilot, starting on a Thursday and Friday and continuing the next Monday to Friday. Nobody in Hollywood works on the weekend.

We did the first two days and I thought, "Fuck. I had no idea it was this hard to do a television show."

We were there all fucking day. And I'm the point man on a single-camera shoot. I'm in every scene. And I don't know what I'm doing.

So all these trained actors are going, "Jeesus Christ, has he ever had a fucking acting lesson?"

Betty would yell, "Cut! Ron, what are you doing?"

"I don't know what I'm doing, Betty. Acting?"

"Well, whatever it is, stop it."

She was such a commanding presence. She made it work. I loved her. There was no question who was in charge. There was one time the assistant director, a guy named Pat, said, "Next time you come around the corner, hug it a little tighter, 'cause I'm losing you in the shot."

Betty goes, "Hey, Pat, how about I direct the fucking actors?" She was salty.

My wife, Barbara, and I were dating then, and she wanted to come out to see me for the weekend. Now, Barbara and I drink together. So I tell her, "You know what, you can come out, but I have all this work to do. I gotta take it easy. I'm exercising. My weight's down. I look good. I don't want to bloat up for the cameras."

She says, "Fine. We'll do what you gotta do."

She arrives late Friday night, but I'm passed out from all day on the shoot. She gets in bed, I don't even wake up. We spend Saturday together real quiet. Sunday morning we go to the beach for an exercise walk.

We didn't drink anything Saturday. We didn't feel bad about it either. We didn't drink all fucking day, we're not drunks. That was easy.

We go for a nice long walk on Manhattan Beach, get our exercise. There's a restaurant there called the Rockfish. We go in there, and we think it really wouldn't kill us if we shared a glass of wine. One small glass of wine with two straws. A little fragment of wine. What would that hurt? No one could be hurt by that. That ain't even drinking, really, just a little sip of wine.

So the waitress comes over to take our order. Barbara says, "I'll have a glass of white wine." And I say, "I'll have a double Johnnie Walker Black on the rocks with a splash of water."

Manhattan Beach is where my buddy from the Blue Collar Comedy Tour, Bill Engvall, lives. So we call his wife, Gail, and she says, "I'm at the airport now, I'm picking Bill up. Where are you?"

"We're at the Rockfish."

"We'll be there in fifteen minutes."

So the waitress comes out and Barbara says, "I'll have another glass of white wine. What about you, Ron?"

"Well, I'll have another double Johnnie Walker Black with a splash of water. That'll be fine."

We're not drinking seriously or anything. We're just waiting for our friends. We're grown-ups, we can have a couple of drinks if we want to.

Gail and Bill show up. Well, Bill makes a lot of money, and he orders a bottle of Opus. I don't drink wine, so I order another double Johnnie Walker Black. They drink the bottle of Opus. We share a salad. Bill orders another bottle of Opus. We're getting trashed, we're getting shit-faced.

Bill and Gail say, "Why don't you come over to our house and party?"

"OK."

When we get there, I know where Bill's liquor cabinet is. I go over there and pull out this twenty-five-year-old bottle of Macallan.

Bill says, "Ron, that's kind of a sipping whisky."

"Not tonight, it ain't." I pour this big old glass full of it, and then I knock it over with my elbow and spill about $80 worth of scotch. We go out to the back, Barbara cracks open a bottle of wine, we're all fucked up.

At some point we forget that they're raising children in this house. This isn't just a fucking bar. This is their house. They told us, "If you want to get in the hot tub, we're gonna put the kids to bed, then we'll come back out and join you."

So I'm in the hot tub, rolling a joint. Barbara says, "Do you think I should leave on my panties?" Barbara will get naked on you, if you let her.

"Well, I don't think so. They're see-through anyway. I'm naked." We start making out.

Bill and Gail come out. Bill's got a bathing suit on up to his armpits. And Gail's got on a turtleneck bathing suit. I swear, I never even heard of a turtleneck bathing suit, but it couldn't have covered her up any better. Barbara's titties are floating on the water, I have a hard-on.

So they sit there for about three minutes and then they say, "We're gonna go to bed. You know where your room is, Ron, you guys can spend the night here."

So Barbara and I, whatever happens happens. We go upstairs and crash. And I start thinking, "Fuck, I gotta be on the set. My call's at six fifteen."

It was fairly early when we went to bed, only about 10:30 or so, 'cause we'd been going at it all fucking day long. But I woke up at 4:30 in the morning, and I'm going, "Fuck. We gotta get outta here."

I look at the bed, and it's got blood all over it. And I

look at my jeans, and there's blood all over my fucking jeans. I'm like, "What the fuck happened? Oh, fuck, let's go."

Barbara says, "We can't leave the bloodied sheets at the Engvalls' house."

I'm like, "We got no choice. I gotta be on the set at six fifteen. We'll just sneak out."

We open the door and the alarm goes off: "Ding, ding, ding." We shut the fucking door, jump in the car, and drive. Barbara says, "Wait a minute. I'm missing my earrings and my watch."

It turns out I had fallen on a glass and cut my leg pretty bad. But I didn't realize I was cut, that's how fucked up I was. I just bled all over their house.

I put Barbara on a plane and went back to work. The Engvalls FedExed Barbara her earrings and watch.

And I've never been invited to their house again. Bill would never tell you that he holds that night against me: the bloodstained sheets, the spilled expensive whisky, saying "cocksucker" in front of his eight-year-old, and Barbara and me getting frisky in the hot tub. Not one little bit: "Ron, your behavior was stellar, thank you for coming over. Visit us again soon."

I felt bad about it. I still feel bad about it. But at the

time I was also feeling good about my career. The Blue Collar Comedy Tour is going great. The concert film is in the can at Warner Brothers, and they're saying they're gonna spend $12 million to promote its release in the theaters. 'Cause it's testing through the roof. It's getting great fucking numbers. People love it.

So I think, "Fuck, I got it made. Warner Brothers loves me. And Fox loves me."

Fox is putting me up in this great hotel. And they've rented this BMW for me to drive. I had never driven one before, and I kinda liked it. Now, I know Fox has other shows in development, but I think, "They can't be treating everybody this great. They must love me in particular."

In fact, Fox had done fourteen pilots and they had spent a pile of money on all of them. But mine was a single-camera shoot. And they had to rent lots from Universal, where we could shoot Mexican street scenes. So it was extra-expensive to produce.

They were gonna pick four shows. They had also bought a pilot from NBC called *The Ortegas* that starred Cheech Marin. So it got down to five shows including *The Ortegas* and *Señor White*.

In the meantime Warner Brothers releases *Blue Collar Comedy* in movie theaters. But instead of spending

$12 million on promotion, they spend $600,000, which is less. And they put it in cities where we'd toured a lot and people had seen us live recently, and they needed to be patient, and they weren't.

Warner Brothers pulled the movie out of release and said they were going to put it straight to DVD. At that time Hollywood only brought a DVD out quick when they thought the movie was a dud.

I still thought *Señor White* was gonna make the cut. I went out and bought a $2,000 suit to wear to the party. I thought there's no way they're gonna pick *The Ortegas*, 'cause it sucked. I got a copy and it was terrible. It was really stereotypical.

My show, I never talked down to the Mexicans. I was the fish out of water, they were the geniuses.

My manager saw the pilot for *The Ortegas* and he told this guy at Fox, "This *Ortegas* thing sucks." And the guy said, 'That's the nicest thing anybody's said about it yet.' "

But they thought they could market Cheech Marin. 'Cause what they wound up doing was brainlessly picking the four shows under development that had the four biggest names. One of 'em ended up being decent. But they made six episodes of *The Ortegas*, and they didn't show any of 'em.

And by the way, since Fox is not picking up my show, I've got to vacate that nice hotel room and turn in the BMW they've been paying for. It's time to stop dreaming about being a television star and get back to doing stand-up.

# 8

## ONSTAGE:
### SET 4

I was in Arizona, I was out late. It was a wild night.

I got back to my hotel at 7:30 in the morning. And I went up to the desk to leave a wake-up call for seven o'clock.

And the lady at the desk goes, "Mr. White, it's past seven."

I'm like, "No, the next one. You got another one coming around, don't you? Why don't you just put me on that one? I hear they're running two a day through Arizona now."

Because of the unrest in the Middle East, we're all just a little bit more familiar with the globe than we used to be. I found out yesterday there really is a place called Bumfuck, Egypt.

And the only way to get there is to go up Shit Creek.

You know the ayatollah in Iran died recently. And they were searching desperately for the next ayatollah.

And I suggested they pick that guy they kicked out of the Oak Ridge Boys. Ayatollah Oom Papa Mau Mau.

My brother's a doctor, and my sister's an attorney. And I hate Thanksgiving.

Last year the family's sitting around the dining-room table. And my brother tells a story about all the lives he's saved. My sister tells a story about winning a lawsuit for an orphanage and helping the children.

My mom goes, "Well, Ron, is there anything new with your career?"

And I go, "Yeah, I got a new bit about sticking my pecker in a toaster."

Maybe I should've told my story first.

I was just in New York. I love New York. And I read an article in the paper there, and it said that there were one hundred million rats in the sewers of Manhattan.

And I was thinking to myself, "Why didn't they just kill them while they were counting them?"

One, *thunk*. Two, *thunk*. With a rat hammer.

I don't even know if there is such a thing as a rat hammer. Be handy, though.

Some people took me tubing down the Salt River. I had never gone tubing before.

Twenty-one of us met to go tube the river. We had six ice chests full of beer with the tubes wrapped around them.

We floated down that river drinking beer for six and a half hours.

And I was baffled by this: Not one person had to pee.

Is that normal? I'd like to think my friends wouldn't pee on themselves.

I know I would. That was the best thing about tubing the river. You could just paddle up to somebody you don't even know, talk to him while you're peeing on yourself. That's relaxed right there. If you're floating down a river drinking a beer, peeing on yourself, there's no tension there, is there?

I guess we'd been floating down that river for like an hour, before I realized, well, everybody's just peeing on themselves. Hell, I'll just pee on myself.

Everybody got mad at me.

Of course, I was in a canoe. Standing up.

Not everybody got mad. A couple of people viewed it as a photo opportunity, and I know that because I got their Christmas card last year.

I don't remember it being that cold that afternoon.

I lived in Mexico for a couple of years. And I was in a horrific car crash down there, and I had a metal plate put in my head by a Mexican doctor.

No kidding. And the weird thing was, right before he performed the surgery he said, "Be very careful, this plate is hot."

I did a show in Bowling Green, Kentucky, and you never know, until you're onstage, how much of the crowd you can see. Usually you might be able to see the first couple of rows.

Or maybe not. But this time I could, and there was a lady in the front row that was wearing a denim western skirt with buttons up the front.

Except it wasn't buttoned up the front. And her legs were just kind of splayed, right?

I'm trying to ignore it, but I've got this shitty attention span that I treat with scotch. Unsuccessfully.

Anyhow, I was so distracted I actually stopped the show, and I said, "Ma'am, would you please close your legs? I can see your slip there."

And she got all pissed off. She goes, "It's not a slip. It's a petticoat."

I'm like, "Well, I can see the junction. And Uncle Joe needs a shave."

Last year I did a show for the troops at Fort Polk, Louisiana. And it was a lot of fun.

But you didn't have to be in the military to be at this show. There were civilians there too.

And I was just talking about the base, and I mentioned, because I toured it that day and I had just learned this, that there were forty thousand men stationed there.

And this really well-dressed drunk woman hollers out, "Every one of them is a bad fuck."

I was like, boy, you know, it seems like after about thirty-nine thousand times you'd start to think, "Maybe it's me. Maybe I need to read a book."


I drink too much. Other people learn things when I drink. Last night a limo driver learned if I say I gotta yak, it doesn't mean I have a long-haired buffalo living in my backyard.

He's like, "Really, what do you feed it?"

"Corn."

The space shuttle depresses me. How big a piece of shit is that piece of equipment?

Good Lord, give them a goddamn tool kit, for fuck's sake. They're out there with a bottle of putty and a spackle blade, trying to put this piece of shit back together.

Well, what are they gonna give them next year, a carrot peeler and some hemostats?

I may be the stupidest son of a bitch that ever lived. I may be. But I thought when the space shuttle blew to smithereens and killed a bunch of people, I thought they were building new ones.

They're not. They're just using the only one they've got left. Folks, this is a 1985 *Columbia*. What do you think the Blue Book is on an '85 *Columbia*?

And I'm not a scientist, but I've got a little tip for the people up at NASA. Quit building the heat shield out of fuckin' foam. It ain't a durable product. A buddy of mine came over the other day, sat on my ice chest, and it busted to pieces. I'm like, that's what's going wrong with the space shuttle right there.

You need something more durable than foam. Like wood.

My uncle came over my house the other day. He used to be president of the Southern Baptist Convention. His name is Dr. Charles Pollard.

And I was making myself a drink. 'Cause I drink in front of anybody. It doesn't matter to me. I don't pretend to be somebody I'm not.

My uncle said, "You're never going to find the answer to your problems in that bottle."

I said, "I know. That's why I'm gonna buy another one. I knew this one was a dud as soon as I opened it."

But it's a sin to waste.


I've been spending a ton of time in Los Angeles. I learn things when I go to L.A.

I learned this: They have bikinis now made out of seashells. I didn't know that.

And I also didn't know this: If you're ever walking down the beach, and you see a girl dressed in a bikini made out of seashells, and you pick her up and hold her to your ear, you can hear her scream.

Who'da thunk it? I thought I'd hear the ocean, but not over that woman.

"Hush, ma'am."

She was a wiggler.

L.A. changes people, that's why I don't like it, you know what I mean? I got a buddy of mine from Houston, a comedian, moves to L.A. Six months in L.A., I don't know him.

Six months in L.A., now he's a vegetarian, a humanitarian, environmentalist. You know, great. If you're a vegetarian, you're not gonna recruit me. I did not climb to the top of the food chain to eat carrots.

It's not even that good for you. Ever see a healthy-looking vegetarian? They look like shit. They're all plump and gray, because their bodies have become intolerant of things they need.

I'll give you an example. My buddy and I were on the way to the Melrose Improv in Hollywood to do a set. And he says this, and I quote, "I feel nauseous and I have a headache. I think that vegetable soup I had for lunch must've had beef broth in it."

I didn't know what to say. "Your system's kicking back—broth? You're a manly man, aren't ya? Why are you a vegetarian?" I asked him.

And it wasn't even because meat was bad for you. He said that raising cattle was bad for the planet, with "cow flatulence in the ozone and the clearing of land for the raising of cattle. What are you doing to help the environment?"

"I'm eating the cows. But I'm only one man."

Every time I read an article in the newspaper in Los Angeles, I get pissed. 'Cause things don't have to make sense in L.A. I read an article in the paper in L.A. that said they were going to try to outlaw the big-screen real-live-handgun-shooting video games. Because they say that that's what's wrong with the youth of America today. They're learning to accurately shoot guns with video games.

It's not a parenting problem, oh no. It's a video problem. They figured it out; congratulations.

Doesn't that piss you off when they have a genuine problem and they try to tack a solution to it that has nothing to do with the problem? It's a parenting problem.

I came up with a great idea. Don't outlaw those machines, give them to the state troopers of California. 'Cause they're some of the worst shots I've ever seen in my life. I saw a shootout once live on TV that went on for so long, eventually the criminal got frustrated and just shot himself.

And the cops are on TV whining about it going, "He's got on body armor, he's got on body armor." I'm watching it live on CNN going, "I can see his head. Shoot him in the head. Give my kid a shot."

"How's that, Daddy?"

"Good shot, Poot. Everybody relax, Poot took him out. Thank God Poot was there."

Horrible shots, some cops are. You ever see that tape of the Kehoe brothers from Ohio, those guys that get out of that white Suburban? They showed it on *COPS* a couple of times.

These guys have a shootout with the police at point-blank range. Nobody gets hurt.

I would love to have been at the office the next day when that guy's being interviewed by the chief.

"And then what happened?"

"Well, at that point I unloaded my semiautomatic nine millimeter weapon at point-blank range."

"And then what happened?"

"They left."

"Nice shooting, Elmer Fudd."

There was a kid in Detroit three years ago shot eight bullets, hit nine people. These two cops shot twenty-two bullets, didn't even hit the fucking Suburban.

Give those guys a roll of quarters, drop 'em off at the mall. That's all I'm saying.

California is just not like Texas, you know? I'll tell you the biggest difference between Texas and California. In Texas we have the death penalty, and we use it.

That's right. If you come to Texas and kill somebody, we will kill you back. That's our policy. We're trying to send a message to the rest of America. And the message is, go somewhere else and kill people. Go to California, they don't give a shit.

I was watching a case on Court TV when I was out there. I got so mad, steam was shooting out of my ears. This guy's convicted of a triple homicide. This guy kills a grandmother, a mother, and a granddaughter without provocation.

The crime's so heinous, I can't even fit it in my head. He's sentenced to death by a jury of his peers, and right before it comes time to carry out the sentence a group of people on his behalf—ON HIS BEHALF—stand up and they go, "We can't kill him, he's too crazy to know we're killing him."

Then what the hell are we arguing about? If he don't know the difference and it makes me feel better . . .

How do you know he's crazy? That's what I want to know. 'Course he's crazy, he killed three people, you know.

This is what they said: "He rolls his turds into little balls and eats crayons." I'm like, shit, they got to quit putting all crazy people in one group, goddamn it. They got to separate them up a little bit, you know what I mean?

"What does that crazy person do?"

"Oh, he rolls his turds into little balls and eats crayons."

"Fine, I'll feed him for the rest of his life. What does that crazy person do?"

"Oh, he kills productive members of our society."

"Well, he should've rolled his shit into little balls and ate crayons. 'Cause the penalty is much less severe."

They're trying to pass a bill right now through the Texas legislature that'll speed up the process of execution in heinous crimes where there's more than three credible eyewitnesses. If more than three people saw you do what you did, you don't sit on death row for fifteen years, Jack, you go straight to the front of the line. Other states are trying to abolish the death penalty, my state's putting in an express lane.

I did that bit out in California. And this guy comes up to me after the show, and you could tell he was nervous to talk to me.

And he goes, "You know what, that may be true about Texas and the death penalty. But you know what, you know what?"

"What?" He waited for me to say what. That's kind of cute.

He goes, "There's an old law in Texas that states that in Texas you cannot shoot somebody in the back, no matter what they did to you or your family or your place of business. It's illegal for you to in turn shoot them in the back."

I went, "Yeah, but you can start shootin' them in the leg till they turn around. 'Cause eventually they're going to get curious."

"Who's shooting me in the leg?" I wonder quietly to myself.

*Oh, that guy.*

Never turn around.

I got thrown out of a bar in New York City. Now, when I say I got thrown out of a bar, I don't mean somebody asked me to leave and we walked to the door together and I said, "Bye, everybody, I gotta go."

Six bouncers hurled me out of a nightclub like I was a Frisbee. Those big old bouncers that go home every night, watch *Road House*, and beat off, you know what I'm talking about?

"Patrick Swayze's hitting another guy, hee-hee-hee."

For wearing a hat. I walk into a bar with a hat on, this guy's real pissy. He goes, "Take off the hat!"

I'm like, "What's the deal?"

He goes, "I'll tell you what the deal is. Faggots in this area wear hats. We're trying to keep 'em out of our club."

"Oh, really? The only way we can tell down South is if they have their hair cut like—yours." And he got all pissed, but he walked away and I took the hat off. And like an hour later, I'd been drinking and I forgot.

You ever forget? It happened to me. I put the hat back on, the guy comes over to me. Now, I'm between 6'1" and 6'6", depending on which convenience store I'm leaving. I weigh 235 pounds. This guy comes over to me, poking me in the shoulder with two fingers, and says, "You're out of here."

I was like, "I don't think so, Scooter." And I was wrong.

They hurled my ass. And then they squared off with me in the parking lot. And I backed down from the fight, 'cause I don't know how many of them it would have taken to whip my ass. But I knew how many they were gonna use.

271

That's a handy little piece of information to have right there—overkill. Well, they called the police, 'cause we broke a chair on the way out the door, and I refused to pay for it.

I refused to pay for it, because "we" broke it over "my" thigh.

The cops showed up. And at that point, I had the right to remain silent . . . but I didn't have the ability.

Cop says, "Mr. White, you are being charged with 'Drunk . . . in . . . Public.' "

I was like, "Hey, hey, hey, hey, I was drunk in a bar. They *threw* me into *public*. I don't want to be drunk in *public*. I want to be drunk in a bar, which is perfectly legal. Arrest them."

Well, he didn't arrest them. Instead he made me do a field sobriety test where you stand on one foot, raise the other foot six inches off the ground, and count to thirty. I made it to "Whoo. Is that gonna be close enough?"

Well, it wasn't close enough, so they call in for my arrest record. There's some good news. Satellites are linking up in outer space, computer banks at NASA are kicking on. There's a telegraph in Fritch, Texas, going, "Beep-beep, beep-beep-beep-beep, dot, deet-deet-deet, dash, dippity, deet-deet-deet, duppety,

deet-deet-deet, dot, dash"—this part takes a while—
"deet-deet-deet, dippety, dot-dot, dash . . . beep."

Now I told you that story to tell you this story:
When I was seventeen years old I was arrested for being drunk in public. Seems to be a pattern.

If you knew Morse code, you'd already know that.

And one DWI, which was a bogus charge, because
it turns out they were stopping every vehicle traveling
down that particular sidewalk. And, hell, that's profiling, isn't it? Profiling is wrong.

On the drunk in public charge in Fritch, the arresting officer, who I had literally known all my life, you know what I mean? This guy lived four doors down from me in a town of less than four hundred people. We've met.

I mean, Fritch was so small, one year our high school marching band made a period. Two years later, they made a comma. They were kicking ass.

Anyhow, the cop who grew up four doors down from me takes me to jail, and when we get there he asks me if I have any aliases. I was just being a smartass, and I said, "Yeah, they call me Tater Salad."

Seventeen years later in New York City, I'm handcuffed on a bench with blood coming out of my nose. And this cop goes, "Are you Ron 'Tater Salad' White?"

"You caught me, you caught the Tater. You can take down those roadblocks now."

# 9

# BACKSTAGE:
## ON THE ROAD AGAIN

Five years ago I was insolvent, with no hope of ever becoming solvent. I had huge tax debts, my financial matters were in fucking disarray, the IRS was on my ass. I had no idea how I'd ever get out of debt. And I really believed that I would die broke.

I was living in my friend Sammy's attic, after coming back from Mexico. And genuinely, from the bottom of my heart, I did not think I would be a success. I thought it would all pass me by, like it passes a lot of people by.

You know, I saw success happen to Foxworthy with my very eyes. I saw him go from headlining small comedy clubs to selling out theaters and arenas and playing the biggest rooms in Las Vegas. It's a huge leap to go from headlining clubs to selling out theaters. Very few comedians ever make it.

I never even thought of that happenin' to me. I really saw myself as kind of like Willie Nelson's harmonica player. I was gonna be back there behind Jeff just blowing on that harp, making a good living doing my job. I was a journeyman comedian doing his thing; I was trying to add more value to Jeff's shows. Jeff paid me real good money, so I made more money than most people. And I would've been doing fine, if it weren't for all my debts.

But all of a sudden, something popped.

I happened to have stuck with it long enough. I wouldn't quit. So when it did catch, I was still there. I'd done the work.

If it catches, it can catch big. The top comedians earn rock-show cash, but a comedian doesn't have ten fucking eighteen-wheelers full of lights and sound and other overhead to pay for. So the lists of the biggest entertainment acts in the country can be a little misleading. They don't really tell you which performers are taking home the most money, because the musicians have so much higher overhead.

The *Blue Collar Comedy Tour: The Movie* DVD is what made it catch for me. Like I said earlier, that was a thing where we all thought it was gonna be huge, when Warner Brothers was saying they were gonna spend $12 million promoting it in movie theaters. Then we all thought it was gonna be nothing, when they only spent $600,000, and pulled it out of the theaters real fast, and sent it straight to DVD.

And then Comedy Central showed it, and it was their highest-rated show ever, and the DVD became a phenomenon. That was kind of the ultimate vindication of the vision Jeff Foxworthy had when he started the Blue Collar Comedy Tour in the first place. He always knew it could be bigger than anybody else ever thought.

Before Warner Brothers downsized the marketing budget on *Blue Collar Comedy Tour: The Movie*, Jeff was the first one to get a copy of the final cut. He called me and said, "I've got it, if you want to see it."

So I went over to his house and he gives it to me, and he says, "This is gonna make you a star. And I'm gonna tell you this one time: Be nice to everybody."

I said, "OK, I will." Now, that was a lie, because I can be an asshole. But I try to be nice.

Jeff is genuinely generous with his time and his effort and his money. He helped me again and again, as I've said. He saw that I was killing myself with drugs and alcohol in the clubs, and he wanted to get me out. He told me one time, "You know what, God's gonna take you one day under the I've-Seen-Enough clause."

He took me off the road and gave me a better place to do stand-up comedy for a period of time. And he gave me a better example of somebody who is gracious, even though they're making a bigillion dollars. He's nice to everybody.

He gives a huge amount of time and energy to Duke Children's Hospital. It's not just lip service or a bunch of money. He goes down every year for four days from Thursday to Sunday for their big fund-raising event. It's a ton of work.

They call me and I'm like, "I'll sign a cap."

But I do enjoy giving them money. Last year in the charity auction they had this fishing trip with Curtis Strange on his boat. He's a Wake Forest guy and lives in Wilmington. I went in there and this group of six guys had the high bid with like $3,000. I said $4,000. I was at lunch, and they called me, said the bid was $6,000. I said $10,000. They bid $11,000, and I said $15,000 and that took it.

But I never had time to do it. I thought of calling him up and saying, "Let's just play golf." I play golf, I don't go deep-sea fishing.

One time when I was opening for Jeff, we're doing two shows on a Saturday night in Reno, Nevada, and Father's Day is the next day, and Jeff wants to get home for that. Well, that's rough, if you're doing two shows in Reno, which is west of Los Angeles, and you get on a plane flying east, losing all of those hours, and you want to be at church the next morning.

The limo's waiting, I've ordered him some food. 'Cause Jeff would forget about himself. He'd get on the plane and go, "Man, I'm starving," and fall asleep. So I'd ordered a sandwich or something for him.

In the audience in Reno there was this kind of

retarded lady who ironed clothes at the Hilton in Las Vegas. And I'd worked that club with Jeff; it's a 1,500-seater that Elvis played a million times. He set the record for 360 sold-out shows there.

And I see this retarded lady walking over to him, and she's got a picture and a pen. And Jeff stopped and talked to her for fifteen minutes. He asked her about her family and made her feel special. Then he said, "Let's get out of here." But while he was talking to that lady, he gave her his full attention.

That's the kind of thing he modeled for me.

One thing's for sure, it's a whole lot better for me to be trying to imitate Jeff's behavior, than for Jeff to be imitating mine. About ten years ago, when Jeff first started hitting it big, he took me on tour with him as his opening act.

The first gig of the tour, our first gig together ever, was in this 900-seat room at the MGM Grand. And Bill Engvall was opening for Reba McEntire at Caesars Palace. They're doing one show a night in this 15,000-seat theater, and we're doing three shows a night in this 900-seat room.

Bill does his show, and then he comes over to see Jeff and me. At that point, I hadn't really spent any time with Jeff in about two years, and I hadn't seen Bill in three years.

And I've come to Vegas with a woman I can't stand. And she can't stand me either, really. Which happened to me a lot back then. The only thing that kept my relationships together was mutual hate.

*"I would rather be miserable than to see you happy with somebody else."*

*"That goes double for me."*

Anyway, after the last show this woman and I go up to our hotel room. And I just wanna go out with Bill and Jeff and throw darts and tell stories and whatever. And I know she's gonna be pissed, she's drunk on red wine.

And I tell her, "Honey, I just wanna go hang out with Jeff and Bill—I haven't seen 'em in a while—and just, you know, go knock back a couple of Co-Colas."

"Fine. Just leave me here in the hotel room by myself then."

"OK, honey, great. See you later."

So Jeff, Bill, and I go out together. And we're playing blackjack and craps. We're winning money. We're telling lies and stories. We're having a blast. It gets to be about 4:30 in the morning, we break it up.

Now, Vegas will make you horny, if you let it. I go back to the hotel room. I'm horny. She's a gorgeous woman, she's laying there in her negligee. But I know if I wake her up, she's gonna hit me in the head with her bucket of nickels.

The only thing that's gonna happen if I wake this girl up to try to have sex with her is that I'm gonna end up with a new mug shot. That's what's gonna happen.

So I think, shit, I'll just do it myself. So I rummage around in the dark, and I find some lotion.

The next morning I wake up. She's making coffee. And she asks me, "What's wrong with your hand?"

I look at my hand. It's dark orange. Bain de Soleil Self Tanning Lotion for Dark Skin Only. And apparently I was getting down, because it was on my nipples and the inside of my thighs and behind my ears.

To be where I am now, ten years later, is amazing. This is such a gratifying time in my career. I've made my own leap from touring the comedy clubs for more than fifteen, almost twenty years, to being able to sell out big theaters. The eight minutes or so of "Tater Salad," somebody told me, is the single most downloaded piece of comedy in the history of the Internet.

My retirement plan was always, "Maybe something neat will happen." And it did. I don't feel like I deserve it especially, but it's still a blast.

One of the great things about being really successful is you have the money to get things working right. Although it can take a little trial and error.

Transportation, for instance. I started out driving to gigs in a beat-to-shit 1986 Nissan pickup. It had a bench vinyl seat that would just bend you over the wheel after about fifty miles. And I'm driving five hundred miles or more at a stretch in between gigs.

And I'm driving places I've never been and wouldn't want to go to at that time of year. That's when I learned you can't be going up to these places like Minnesota and Wisconsin in the wintertime with some Texas jackets. You need to have special shit. Or you will freeze your ass right off.

Early on as a comedian I was performing in Green Bay, Wisconsin, and they're having this horrendous cold snap. It was colder than anything I'd ever experienced. It's like forty below, and I mean it's so bad that I can't get from the apartment to the cab to go to work without being in pain.

And I don't have the special shit you need to survive in that weather. I just went up there with some Texas jackets. And I was dying. And I thought, well, there's not gonna be anybody there.

The place was packed. They put on their same outfit they wear to the Packers game, and they wore it over to the comedy club. They got a huge coatroom for all the snowsuits and parkas and shit.

These people put on their cold-weather gear in late

October, and they take it off about April. Which you can appreciate, if you've ever been up there with 'em during that time.

Smells like it too. Which you can appreciate, if you've ever been up there with 'em during that time.

You put on all those layers, and you heat up. It's only natural.

What's that fragrance? Eau de Parka. Eau de Long Johns.

Another time I had a gig in Omaha to get to. I called the club, and said I was on my way. I'd played this club before, and the girl who answered the phone, Mimi, said, "Oh, great, Ron. We're waiting for you. We've been looking forward to having you back."

I get outside and my truck won't start. So I catch a Greyhound bus. It's January and it starts to snow, and we get stuck behind a jack-knifed Little Debbie's tractor-trailer. I'm sitting in the front of the bus, staring at this eighteen-wheeler, thinking, "I wonder if this bus has got a tool kit with a tire iron. We could bust into that Little Debbie's truck, and at least I could get something to eat." Because I hadn't had anything to eat, and I didn't have any money, and I was starving.

They finally get things cleared up, we chug along to the next stop, which is Kansas City. I call the club to tell 'em I'm gonna be late, and they tell me, "You're here *next* week." So the next Tuesday I had to make the trip all over again.

Then I got to where I could buy a custom van to tour in. And now I fly, or most of the time I travel on a custom tour bus. My wife, Barbara, and I have paid our dues with tour buses, let me tell you.

The first time Barbara and I rented a bus, the bus company sent us a goddamn band bus that sleeps twelve people in bunks, with a single bed and a couch in the back. Barbara and I can't even sleep together, and we're gonna be on this bus for twenty-two nights.

I get on the bus and I think, "These fuckin' people knew what I wanted. They knew it was just me and my wife, and they go ahead and give us this huge band bus that we can't use."

And I'm paying top dollar for a bus and a driver. So I get on the phone and I'm just fucking cussin' out this guy at the bus company. They tell me they got another bus for us, a Star Coach, we're gonna love it. And we're supposed to rendezvous with this new bus and shift into it.

Well, they didn't have a driver available that had ever operated this Star Coach. What they found was this guy named C.B., who had to be seventy years old and didn't weigh a hundred pounds. As we found out later, he had driven eighteen-wheelers for forty years.

And then he got a job driving these fifty-five-seat Blue Bird buses that church and school groups rent to go on outings. And then he started driving for this company we were renting the tour bus from.

Well, old C.B. had plenty of driving experience, no doubt about that. But they put him on this super-modern, custom coach that's so fancy, it's got push-button everything. You need to take a class to learn all the controls.

As soon as I got on the bus, I had to take a piss. The door's open to the bathroom. I walk in, I turn around, and there's this six-button panel. I push a button and the door closes. "OK," I think, "cool." I turn around and take a piss. I turn back around, and—I don't have my glasses—I push a button, and the lights go out.

Now I'm in the dark, I can't see shit, I'm pushing all these buttons, and I can't get out. I'm going, "This fucking sucks. Hey! Hey!"

Well, it turns out you need to push the same button twice. But if you don't know that, you're gonna push all the other buttons, and then start kicking shit. And you're still trapped.

It was a pretty bus, but dirty. But it was a nicer bus than the first one they sent us. It was all one big salon in the back with a nice bed.

By the time we've made this detour to shift into

the new bus, it's gotten late. Barbara and I are exhausted, so we go in the back and go to bed. I had ridden on a custom tour bus once before, and the ride was incredibly smooth. I slept like a baby. So that's what I'm expecting now.

C.B. puts the bus into gear and gets on the highway. *Bang, bang, bang.* Barbara and I are bouncing off the bed. It's so fuckin' rough, we can't believe it. *Bang, bang, bang, bang.*

It turns out with these buses, when you park 'em, you let the air out of these hydraulic lifts and they sit way down low on the ground. Well, C.B. didn't know that. We're hearing all these appalling grinding noises, we're bouncing a foot off the bed, and I'm going, "This can't be right."

It wasn't near as bad up at the front, but it wasn't too good, either. C.B.'s holding on valiantly. I say, "You know what, it's a little rough back there."

C.B. pulls over at a gas station, we go out and look at the bus. The mud flaps are laying flat on the fucking ground. I go, "You know what, I don't know anything about these buses, but I know for a fact that the mud flaps don't drag on the ground."

Well, we've got truckers and everything trying to figure out the system to get this bus off the ground. We get the front end up, but not the back end. You gotta know how to operate that specific bus, because they're all different. They're all made and customized by different people.

Eventually we get it off the ground. Now it's driving so much better, Barbara and I can finally relax and get a little sleep. In the morning C.B. pulls into a Cracker Barrel for us to go eat. We don't know this guy, but we can tell he's a character.

We have this awkward moment, because we don't know if we're supposed to invite him to join us or if he goes off and eats with other bus drivers who happen to be there or whatever. So there's this awkward pause, and then I go, "Come eat breakfast with us."

We sit down at the table, and C.B. says, "Do you like pickles?"

"Yeah, I like pickles fine."

"Let me tell you a story about pickles. I drove eighteen-wheelers for forty years, and I was out in Los Angeles, California, and I pulled my truck up to the dock to unload. And I'm gonna have to drive back empty all the way to Atlanta, and I make no money at all for that. And I notice there on the loading dock there are cases and cases of pickles."

Barbara and I are leaning in to get all the details now. We never heard a pickle story before.

"I asked the ole boy who was working the dock. I said, 'What's the deal with the pickles?'

"The ole boy said, 'Onst a month, we sell our employees pickles at discount prices.'

"I said, 'Well, you know what, I'm kind of an employee. I'm working right here on your loading dock, after all.'

"He said, 'Well, you know what, we've got so many pickles, we'll sell you pickles at employee prices.' Do you know what I did?"

We said, "No, what did you do?"

"I bought every pickle on the dock. And I loaded my truck up with 'em, and I took off across America selling pickles. I met one woman that was having a pickle party. Have you ever heard of a pickle party?"

"No."

"She bought four cases of pickles. I paid four dollars a case, I'm selling 'em for nine dollars a case. You think I wasn't making money?"

He tells the story in such a manner that I think he's still got a few cases of pickles left that he wants to sell me. It turns out this happened thirty years ago.

"I stopped at grocery stores. I told 'em, 'I got pickles at discount prices. What kinda pickles you want?' And they stocked the shelves."

He was Johnny Pickleseed, I guess.

C.B. drove for us for a while. Now, our dogs have never chewed up anything. But if C.B. left anything out on the bus, our dogs would chew it up. They chewed up his glasses, his cigarettes, his phone book.

He's actually calling the bus company saying, "I've got another pair of glasses in my house. You're gonna need to FedEx 'em to me." He's driving the bus blind.

He's got this black bag he always carries with him. One day it's open, and I look inside, and he's got nine bottles of pills in there. And I'm like, "What the fuck is wrong with this guy?"

He was a sweet guy, and he wasn't a bad driver. Once he got it going, he kept it going smooth.

Then one time we were driving up north, going 70 mph into a 70 mph headwind. So we have a relative 140 mph wind, and we start hearing a rumble that wakes me up in the back going, "What the fuck is happening?"

We stop the bus, we don't see anything. We start up again, everything seems OK. But as soon as we get up some speed, we hear that rumble again. We've got eight hundred miles to drive.

Then we figure from the sound that it's got to be something on the top of the bus. We stop at a little gas station next to an abandoned motel in the middle of nowhere. And the gas station guy says, "My brother's an electrician. And he's got an electrical truck with a bucket on the back of it parked right over there. He's using the bathroom right now, but I bet he'll let you use it."

They know who I am and they say, "Oh, yeah, let's try to get this fixed." They find the problem—a spotlight on the top of the bus that was wrenched around the wrong way. Part of it had come loose, and if you were going more than 30 mph, it would start to clatter and shake. They bungee-cord the spotlight down so it won't vibrate or shake. And we're good to go.

In the fall of 2004 that electrician got married, and his mother e-mailed me on my Web site to tell me about it. I showed up at the reception in Indiana as a surprise; I had the charter plane land in this little airport, and they were shocked and delighted to see me there. And it was just such a pleasure to be able to go pay my respects to somebody who had helped me out of a jam.

Back to C.B., we liked him fine. But we were worried about his health, not just driving the bus, but dealing with repairs and other problems along the way.

Then we got this fellow, call him Fred, who'd been

driving rock 'n' rollers for a long time. But he wasn't a good driver. We didn't know. We were falling all over the place, and we thought that's just how it was. I figured he's avoiding sniper fire.

Whenever we'd get somewhere and there was luggage to be moved or anything like that, Fred would get on his cell phone and just wander off. You wouldn't know where he was. Barbara and I would have to lug our shit.

I got to thinking Fred's days as our driver were numbered. I'd confronted him about all the things I didn't think he was doing well, although he was being very well paid, but I didn't think he wanted to try to improve his performance for us.

We're on the bus heading home to Atlanta, and Barbara and I have two friends with us. I pour everybody some Johnnie Walker Blue Label. Then I don't know for what reason, but Fred slams on the brakes and about $140 worth of scotch goes flying forward and splattering over everybody. And in my head I'm going, "He's gone. He spilled my goddamn booze."

And then our current and forever driver, Todd, showed up like Superman: "Bomp-da-da-bom! I'll take care of every problem you've got. I'll drive your bus and never spill a drop. I'll carry every bag you've ever seen." That's not what he said, mind you, that's what he's done.

The first time Todd drove for us, we left a bottle of wine on the marble countertop in the tour bus galley. We weren't trying to test the new driver, we just forgot about it. The next morning I see that bottle in the exact same place. I can't believe it. And I mention this to Todd, and he says real matter-of-fact, "That's why the other guy isn't here anymore. And I am."

Todd grew up on a farm in Iowa, and he is one of those quiet, incredibly competent people who never panics in a crisis. He can drive anything, and he can fix anything he can drive. Barbara and I say that we want Todd to be the highest-paid bus driver in America, because he's the best bus driver in America.

You oughta see Todd drive a bus. I've never ever seen him start into a turn he couldn't make. He's never backed it up twice.

We were going to a NASCAR race one time, and there's a wreck on the freeway. That's gonna be bad anyway, but if it's 140,000 people trying to go to one spot, it's hell.

And Todd backs this bad big ole bus up through traffic and finds a way using his computer and navigation system to go a back way through this residential area. And eventually he's got thirty cars behind him. The drivers all figure, "Well, that guy knows where the fuck he's going, let's follow him."

On the way home from the race, we're stuck in traffic again. And a car catches on fire. But it's not on the same road where we're stuck. And Todd goes out with his cell phone, calls the fire department, directs the fire department in. He comes back to the bus—my ex-wife, Terry, and her husband were with us, they're good friends of ours—and Terry goes, "He's probably gonna deliver a baby on the way back."

Barbara and I sleep like babies in the bus because we know Todd is the best. If something bad happens, Todd will do the most that can be done.

He drives us everywhere at home too. 'Cause I drink too much, I shouldn't drive a lot of the time.

He does so much stuff for us, I hired him to work for Barbara and me full-time. He takes care of all our cars. If we go on a vacation, he looks after the house and the dogs. The dogs love him. They know he's family.

And on the road, he's become my tour manager as well as bus driver. If there is a problem, he fixes it. He is totally trustworthy. Our goal is to keep him with us, even if we stop needing him to drive the tour bus.

But I guarantee you, Todd was born to drive. When

he was three years old, I'm sure he was going around the house with a dinner plate pretending he was driving.

Todd's building us a black stretch limo that will seat nine people, for less than it would cost to buy a Ford Taurus. He found one car in Atlanta for the mechanicals and chassis and another in Kentucky for the body.

All my vehicles are black. The tour bus—we call it the Tater Wagon—is a beautiful black Prevost custom coach with a decal wrap of a cigar in an ashtray on the back and cigar smoke on the sides. It's just like the wraps they put on NASCAR racers, with all the sponsors' logos. If you want to change it, you just peel it off.

I've got a black Lincoln Blackwood truck that I bought before I really hit it big. I couldn't afford it, but I just had to have it. I'd come home and go for a drive in that truck, just smilin'. I couldn't believe it was mine.

The whole truck bed is solid burlwood. It's a chopped Navigator is what it is. They only made two thousand of 'em, so they're really, really rare.

And I've got a black Bentley Flying Spur. I used to have the Bentley Continental GT, but I traded it in for the Flying Spur. It's the fastest production sedan in the world, with a top speed of 190 mph.

I had it up to 135 on the highway once, and it was bored to pieces at that speed. Half the systems in the car hadn't even turned on yet, 'cause that was still too slow for 'em to be needed.

I wanted chrome wheels for the Bentley. The dealer wanted $5,000 for 'em. Todd said, "Wait a minute, that's bullshit. We can have the wheels that are on it chromed for twelve hundred." The next weekend the Bentley's on blocks while Todd's getting the wheels chromed.

I was playing golf with some friends on Monday, and I wasn't expecting the wheels to be ready then. To surprise me, Todd brought the car down with the chromed wheels and parked it at the course so I could drive it home from there. So I finished my round with my buddies, and it was the first time they saw the car, and it looked beautiful. That fuckin' thing was shining. You can read the fine print off a newspaper in the reflection from the thirty coats of paint it's got on it.

Golf has always been one of my favorite things. I started playing when I was fifteen, and there's always a set of clubs on the tour bus. I've got a 14 handicap that I'm always trying to shave a little off of.

On the Blue Collar Comedy Tour sometimes Jeff, Larry, Bill, and I would play foursomes. We even had our own tournament with trophies and everything, the Wannabe Classic, which was just a great excuse for having fun playing bad golf.

I've had the chance over the last few years to play at some great courses, like Augusta National, the home of the Masters Tournament. And I've met a few PGA Tour players, which is a huge kick for me. I've played with Mark Brooks, and I played five holes with Stewart Cink at my home club outside Atlanta. He makes our golf course, which is a very hard course, look like a pitch and putt. He scored 29 on the back nine.

I'm gonna play in the BellSouth Classic Pro-Am this year. I can't go as a fan, because I have to sign so many autographs I don't get to see any of the golf. Inside the ropes those guys are much bigger than I am. Phil Mickelson won the tournament last year in a playoff.

As far as my career goes, I'm in a great place and I'm loving it. The only thing I'm not doing a lot of now, that I'd like to do more of, is television. I've done specials for Comedy Central and the WB network, but I'd really like to do a series.

The special I did for the WB, *The Ron White Show*, was actually meant to be a pilot for a regular variety show, like the old *Dean Martin Show*. The people at the network begged me to do this show. I mean, they begged me. They're just blowing me, trying to get me to say yes.

Actually, I thought it was an easy show to do, you know. 'Cause I don't have to act, I just have to be myself onstage. There's a really talented cast to do skits. It's gonna be filmed in Las Vegas. I like everybody that works on the show.

We did the show, and it went over great. We had an audience of four million, which was bigger than anything the WB usually got. A lot of the television reviews were really positive.

It wasn't the end all to beat all, but if you wanted a little fucking Dean Martin back in your life—an amusing guy onstage with some dancing girls and a scotch—it was fun. It could've found its spot.

And the WB told us they were gonna pick it up as a series. And they told Sony, which was the studio, and Sony went out and spent $2 million to get everything lined up to produce the series in Las Vegas.

Then the WB decided that they were going to shift direction away from *Blue Collar Television*—Jeff, Bill, and Larry's show—and everything associated with it, which included my show. Even though my show, like I said, was closer to Dean Martin than to Blue Collar.

Anyway, they said they weren't going to pick up *The Ron White Show* as a series, and that tore my fuckin' heart out. But the people who were really pissed were the people at Sony Television, 'cause they'd spent a pile of money on the WB's say-so and been made to look like fools.

But I've got another television project that may go. One of the neat things on *The Ron White Show* was we did these animated vignettes of some of my stage bits featuring a cartoon "Tater Salad" version of me. TBS is now developing an animated series, *They Call Him Tater Salad*, based on those vignettes, just like *The Simpsons* came out of those little "Simpsons" vignettes on *The Tracey Ullman Show*.

The Tater Salad character is sort of like Homer Simpson, King of the Hill, or the Family Guy. It'd be great if the animated show gets a chance. I could do the work near home in Atlanta, and I could steer clear of Hollywood.

I guarantee you, I found out Hollywood doesn't want anything new. Hollywood does not want an original idea, or they'd have put on *Señor White*. They say they want something new, they want something 5 percent new. They don't want 95 percent new. They don't know what to do with it. Whatever you want to do, you gotta be able to say it's like something they already succeeded with: "It's like *Northern Exposure*, except it's in Mexico."

That's what we tried—"It's *Southern Exposure*"—and it was a good analogy, actually. But they couldn't see it.

That's a lot of water, and more than a little scotch, under the bridge. If I never get a television series, I'll be OK. I have a great job, great fans, a great life. I love going onstage and making a big crowd laugh, and I hope I get to keep doing that for a long, long time.

# ACKNOWLEDGMENTS

I'd like to thank my manager John MacDonald and all the people at MacDonald-Murray Management for all they do. Maria, thanks for taking care of all the details. John, just remember this was your idea.

I'd like to acknowledge Sandy Fox, Maggie Houlehan, Jeff Abraham, Todd Modderman.

Special thanks to Hilary Hinzmann for his editorial help in putting this book together, and Matthew Shultz for the killer illustrations. Couldn't have done it without you guys.

Thanks to my literary agents David Vigliano and Elisa Petrini for peddling this project.

And thanks to the good folks at Dutton, especially Brian Tart and Mark Chait, for putting my words into print.

# ABOUT THE AUTHOR

Ron White gained fame as part of the Blue Collar Comedy phenomenon, which includes the hit movie *Blue Collar Comedy Tour: The Movie* that has sold over three million DVDs and was a smash hit on Comedy Central. He has since gone on to achieve individual mass appeal with sold-out shows in theaters and arenas; a hit comedy album, *Drunk in Public*; a hit DVD, *They Call Me "Tater Salad,"* which has sold over 1.5 million copies; his latest release, *You Can't Fix Stupid*, a bestseller on both CD and DVD; and top-rated specials on the WB network and Comedy Central. Visit his Web site at www.tatersalad.com.